Developing School Provision for Children with Dyspraxia

Developing School Provision for Children with Dyspraxia

A Practical Guide

Edited by Nichola Jones

P·C·P

Paul Chapman
Publishing

First published 2005

Paul Chapman Publishing
A SAGE Publications Company
1 Oliver's Yard
55 City Road
London EC1Y 1SP

SAGE Publications Inc
2455 Teller Road
Thousand Oaks, California 91320

SAGE Publications India Pvt Ltd
B-42, Panchsheel Enclave
Post Box 4109
New Delhi 110 017

Library of Congress Control Number: 2005924792

A catalogue record for this book is available from the British
Library

ISBN 1-4129-1037-4
ISBN 1-4129-1038-2 (pbk)

Typeset by Pantek Arts Ltd, Maidstone, Kent
Printed on paper from sustainable resources
Printed in Great Britain by Cromwell Press, Trowbridge, Wiltshire

Contents

Lois Addy is a senior lecturer in the School of Professional Health Studies at York St John. She has over 23 years experience as a paediatric occupational therapist having worked in mainstream/special schools and child development centres across the country.

Lois is co-author of the Write from the Start perceptual-motor handwriting programme, published by LDA (UK) Ltd, and *Making Inclusion Work for Children with Dyspraxia: Practical Strategies for Teachers*, published by Routledge Falmer. She is also the author of the Speed-Up! kinaesthetic handwriting programme, and *How to Understand and Support Children with Dyspraxia*, both published by LDA (UK) Ltd. Lois is on the medical committee of the Dyspraxia Foundation and the editorial board of the National Association of Paediatric Occupational Therapists (NAPOT) and is a committee member of the National Handwriting Association.

Sheila E. Henderson began her professional career as a PE teacher. After teaching for a short time she moved into psychology and gained a BA (first class), MA and PhD. In 1974, she took up a Research Lectureship in children with movement disorders at the Institute of Education, University of London where she now works part-time. Supported by research grants from the Medical Research Council, Action Research, Scope and numerous other charities, she has published over 100 monographs and papers in scientific and professional journals and edited volumes. These range in topic from the motor difficulties of children with Downs syndrome to educational concomitants of 'clumsiness', and include experimental studies of normal motor and cognitive development as well as large-scale medical follow-up studies of children at risk. The *Movement Assessment Battery for Children*, of which she is principal author, has been translated into ten languages and has become one of the most widely used measures of developmental coordination disorders in the world. She has lectured on her work throughout Europe, North America and the Far East.

Diane Jenkins is a parent to Dale who attends a comprehensive school in Bridgend and who has been diagnosed with dyspraxia. Diane was instrumental in setting up a parent group for children with coordination difficulties in her local area. She has linked with the local education authority to provide her expertise and input as part of a task group set up to develop services for children with coordination difficulties.

Nichola Jones trained and began her career teaching PE and later specialized in SEN. She is currently the assistant head of an advisory SEN service in Wales. Part of her role has been to help identify, assess and develop differentiated strategies for children with movement difficulties. Nichola was the Welsh president for NASEN and is currently a council member of the General Teaching Council in Wales. She is also a committee member of the National Handwriting Association. Her specific area of interest is in early years where she is currently conducting her PhD research.

Christine Macintyre is an honorary fellow of Edinburgh University. Her first qualification was in physical education, followed by another in Psychology and these merged to give the research background for a PhD in 'The Assessment of Movement'. She now conducts training and consultancy work on all aspects of Early Years, Special Educational Needs and research methods. She has written many books centred on the importance of movement for learning and the impact poor movement has on the intellectual as well as the social and emotional development of children. She lectures at conferences and offers professional development work at home and abroad.

Gavin Reid is a senior lecturer in the Department of Educational Studies, Moray House School of Education, University of Edinburgh. He is an experienced teacher, educational psychologist, university lecturer, researcher and author. He has made over 500 conference and seminar presentations worldwide. He has authored, co-authored and edited twelve books for teachers and parents. He is the author of *Dyslexia: A Practitioners Handbook* (3rd edn, Wiley, 2003), *Dyslexia: A Complete Guide for Parents* (Wiley, 2004), *Dyslexia and Inclusion* (David Fulton/NASEN, 2005) and *Learning Styles and Inclusion*

(Sage Publications, in press). He has also co-authored the *Listening and Literacy Index* (LLI) and the *Special Needs Assessment Profile (SNAP)* (Hodder & Stoughton).

Philip Vickerman is Head of the Centre for Sport at Liverpool John Moores University. He has worked nationally and internationally on the inclusion of children with special educational needs in physical education. Recently Philip advised the DfES on the production of a CD-ROM resource that supports teachers to include children with SEN in PE. Philip regularly carries out training seminars for teachers and support assistants, and has published widely in many books and professional resources.

Barbara Walsh has been involved in education all her life, working firstly in schools as a physical education teacher, then head of department as well as head of year. During this time the main focus in her teaching was to create an environment where success for all was achievable. She moved into higher education several years ago to work with trainee teachers of physical education and to continue with her philosophy for success. Barbara is currently Head of the Centre for Physical Education in the School of PE, Sport and Dance at Liverpool John Moores University.

Children with Development Coordination Disorder: Setting the Scene

Nichola Jones

Over the last decade special educational needs (SEN) has seen an acceleration in the interest and provision that is continuing to emerge in schools in England, Scotland, Wales and Ireland. With a much greater awareness in schools of conditions like dyslexia, dyspraxia and autism, and the effects they have in the context of the educational curriculum, schools are becoming better placed to help children access a curriculum that takes account of the diverse needs of its learners. It has been predicted that as we move through the early years of this millennium mainstream schools will witness significant changes in their practice. 'Inclusion will certainly happen increasingly over the first part of the new century... The desegregation and anti-discriminatory political environment is now international and it seems impossible that its direction will be reversed' (Thomas, 1997, p. 106). Procedures for the identification and assessment of needs have been specified in the Special Educational Needs Code of Practice (SENCOP 2001), while the right to equal opportunities is made clear in the Special Educational Needs and Disability Act (SENDA) 2001.

For children with a developmental coordination disorder (DCD) and other conditions the effectiveness of provision is bound up with a school's ability to optimize learning for all pupils. As Ainscow (1999) points out, the necessary focus for these children is one of whole-school improvement in which teachers are encouraged to reflect critically on establishing procedures for ensuring the educational progress of all students. This approach suggests 'all teachers are teachers of pupils with special educational needs and that teaching these pupils is a whole school responsibility, requiring a whole school approach' (SENCOP 2001). This process engages teachers in providing a differentiated curriculum that gives opportunities for all learners. However, a problem arises where teachers do not have the necessary skills to understand the variety of learning styles in the teaching process, the range of skills children bring with them to the classroom and the types of difficulties they may encounter. The Teacher Training Agency SEN Subject Specialist Standards predicts that 'more teachers in mainstream school will need to acquire the necessary understanding and skills to work effectively with pupils.' The aim of this book is to equip the reader with some of the fundamental skills that are needed to cater for children with DCD. It also seeks to direct professionals working with children to key resources which can help develop teacher competency.

Developmental coordination disorder

As early as 1900 the idea that there might be a discrete childhood syndrome which has 'clumsiness' of movement as its defining symptom began to emerge. In fact, doctors and teachers have been aware of movement difficulties as a significant problem in child development since the beginning of the twentieth century (Henderson and Sugden, 1992, p. ix). Case histories of children who appear physically and intellectually normal yet lack the motor competence necessary to cope with the demands of everyday living are catalogued in the literature (e.g. Brenner and Gillman, 1967; Gubbay, 1975; Henderson and Hall, 1982).

Gubbay (1975) in a comprehensive study used the term 'clumsiness', viewing it as a general condition of impaired ability to perform skilled purposive movements by children who otherwise are mentally normal and without bodily deformity. Gubbay defines clumsiness using the medical terms apraxic and agnostic ataxia. Praxis involves the planning of movements, whereas gnosia is making meaning of sensory input. Ataxis, which is when steady or uncoordinated movement is added, displays itself when a 'clumsy' child may not understand what needs to be done and may not be able to plan, leading to uncontrolled or uncoordinated movement. This book seeks to deepen the understanding of and unlock teacher empathy for the conditions these children present with and find solutions to curriculum accessibility.

Terminology

Many terms including 'clumsy' have been used to describe the condition. These include motor coordination problems, motor impairment, movement difficulties, developmental dyspraxia, minimal brain dysfunction and congenital maladroitness (see Henderson and Barnett, 1998). Most recently the term 'developmental coordination disorder' (DCD) has become influential in highlighting this area, with leading researchers using the term (e.g. Henderson and Sugden, 1992; Wright and Sugden, 1995, 1996). The term DCD appears in both the American Psychiatric Association's (APA) Manual for Mental Disorders (DSM IV), (APA, 1994) and the World Health Organisation (WHO) Classification of Diseases and Related Health Problems (ICD-10) (WHO, 1992).

The essential feature of developmental coordination disorder is described as 'a marked impairment in the development of motor co-ordination (criterion A). The diagnosis is made only if this impairment significantly interferes with academic achievement or activities of daily living (criterion B).'

Prevalence

The prevalence of DCD has been estimated as high as 6 per cent for children in the age range of 5–11 years (APA, 1994). Other studies include Gubbay (1975), Henderson and Hall (1982), Iloeje (1987), Godfrey (1994), Marks (1994) and Portwood (1996), and all indicate a prevalence of between 5–6 per cent. The problem affects more boys than girls in a ratio of 3–4 : 1 (Gordon and McKinlay, 1980). These figures suggest that in every school class there is potentially at least one child with DCD. However, as Wright (1997) points out, there are problems in assessing its prevalence and nature, especially since no assessment procedure has been clearly established, indicating that different tests might identify different groups of children

Diagnosis

There is also a lack of agreement on what is necessary for a child to be categorized as having DCD, and to what extent the condition coexists alongside other 'specific' learning difficulties. Kaplan et al. (1998), who challenge the view of focusing on the symptoms (skill deficits) rather than syndromes, consider the issue of co-morbidity. Kaplan et al.'s research goes on to suggest that there are no pure diagnosis categories of developmental disorders, but rather semi-random clusters of symptoms related to motor coordination, autism, learning and so on. Out of a study measuring 162 children for DCD, reading difficulties and attention deficit hyperactivity disorder (ADHD), 53 children obtained scores which classified them as 'pure' cases, 47 children did not meet the criteria for any of the three conditions and 62 were classified as 'co-morbid' cases. Kaplan et al. suggest co-morbidity is the rule rather than the exception. Schools might then focus on the skills deficit or barriers to learning and how these affect performance and function in the education environment as a way forward for managing groups of children with coordination difficulties.

The idea of focusing on characteristics rather than conditions is explored in Chapter 2, which considers the wider context of a child with specific learning difficulties. The major consideration is that certain aspects of a child's specific difficulties (dyslexia, DCD, dyscalculia) may be presented more prominently at certain times during their school career.

Identification and assessment issues

Structured, formal assessment is a key feature of the National Curriculum, providing an integral part of the educational process and continually providing feedback as well as informing future planning. The Special Educational Needs Code of Practice (SENCOP 2001) outlines how to identify and assess children with special needs and stipulates that the needs of all pupils who have SEN during their school career have to be addressed. The definition of a special need is having a significantly greater difficulty in learning than the majority of children of the same age. However, in the area of assessing children's motor development, there is very little attention received compared to that of the cognitive domain. This problem is cited with the much broader issue concerning the emphasis on the academic disciplines that currently dominate the National Curriculum despite other developments in learning. These include Gardener's Multiple Intelligence Theory (1999), which considers logical, musical, spatial and interpersonal dimensions equally within the learning environment.

Therefore, without any formal motor assessment, it is unlikely that children, particularly those at the less severe end of the continuum, ever reach 'School Action' as prescribed by the Code of Practice (2001). With greater awareness of the important benefits of identifying pupils' difficulties early, it is even more crucial that formal assessment procedures are developed. Such tests should provide baseline information on pupil performance and monitor progress in order that resource allocations within the local authority can be distributed equally for the whole of the specific learning difficulty spectrum. This book will identify some of the tests available that can be used by specially trained teachers.

Children's main difficulties in the education environment

Children with DCD are likely to lack movement skills that the majority of their peers gain automatically (see Fig. 1.1). The movement problems facing children with DCD are well documented (Morris and Whiting, 1971; Stott, Moyes and Henderson, 1984; Van Dellen and Geuze, 1988) and describe the children as being relatively slow and inaccurate in all sorts of perceptual motor skills. They suggest that these children would have difficulty in acquiring such skills as 'constructing models, writing, hopping, cycling and throwing or catching a ball' (p. 489). Dare and Gordon (1970) argue that such children are unable to learn tasks like fastening buttons or tying laces at the appropriate age. Children are rarely good at ball games, and as Sugden and Wright (1996) point out, they may be considered clumsy in either or both fine and gross motor skills.

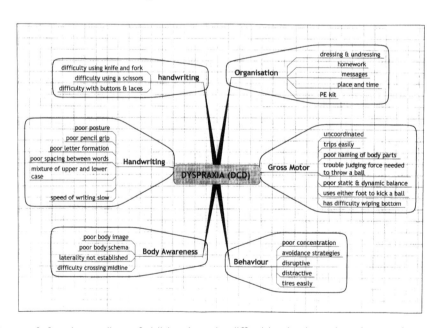

Figure 1.1   An outline of children's main difficulties in the education environment

Studies of children with DCD have also revealed that there is a strong correlation between their poor motor coordination and social and emotional problems. Children's perception of their lack of physical competencies, especially when exhibited among their peers, often results in an unwillingness to participate in a number of activities. Children's lack of confidence in their physical competence can also influence the performance of other activities. Schoemaker and Kalverboer (1994) found that children with movement problems judged themselves to be less competent socially and were more introverted and anxious than their well-coordinated peers. Small-scale teacher research projects in Bridgend County Borough Council reflect that low-level intervention significantly increases self-esteem and has the secondary effect of improving classroom performance (Jones, 2002).

At the other end of the age spectrum it has also been found that teenagers with motor problems are very conscious of their physical difficulties and that this has significant implications for their social and emotional well being (Cantell et al., 1994). Often these problems in motor coordination increase as children are withdrawn or excluded from activities that they are unable to participate in. Support to help pupils take control of their own learning should be considered, particularly with regard to the changes they need to make to participate or to adapting the activity appropriately.

Intervention in school

As long ago as 1975 Gubbay suggested that it was not so important *what* was being done as long as *something* was being done to help these children. The overwhelming conclusion drawn from reviewing the literature on intervention studies for individuals with DCD is that most intervention appears to work but that no specific approach is clearly superior, although the literature supports the need for further research programmes (Peters and Wright, 1999). As Sugden and Sugden (1991) suggest, after parents, teachers are in the best position to provide remediation on a large scale. One form of helping children with motor difficulties is to implement a 'motor programme'. This form of intervention has been emerging across England, Scotland and Wales for pupils with coordination difficulties. Often programmes are administered on a ten-minute daily basis and can be delivered by trained teachers or teaching assistants. In the first instance an assessment is administered to establish a baseline and then a programme is implemented for anything up to 12 weeks. The general outcome of the motor programmes has shown that giving support for the development of motor skills is beneficial, and with minimal training it is possible to deliver an effective intervention, albeit in a discreet, segregated group setting. Motor programmes are explored later in this book to provide ideas on how schools can develop this type of intervention in their local setting.

But to really embed structures that will firmly establish and help design appropriate curriculum opportunities for the diverse needs of pupils with coordination difficulties, schools will need to provide appropriate adaptations as well as the support and training that teaching and support staff will require to deliver a curriculum for all. Two areas that are frequently identified as giving teachers most cause for concern are those of physical education and children's handwriting. These two aspects of the curriculum are considered in more detail along with some of the key issues that schools will need to address in order to provide an all-inclusive environment.

Working in collaboration

SENCOP 2001 emphasizes the important role of external agencies in helping schools identify, assess and make provision for pupils with special needs. Certainly for children with developmental coordination disorder the school doctor, paediatric physiotherapist, occupational therapist and speech and language therapist can play a crucial role in the development of school services for these children. Law et al. (2001) carried out a study looking at how health and education can develop the process of collaboration. The study suggested that to achieve effective collaboration it is vital to have structures in place which enable the setting of common goals. The implication is that a team of people can achieve more together than as individuals. Losen and Losen (1985) use the term 'synergy' to summarize the process.

With the National Service Framework (NSF) for Children and Young People in place this has meant there is great potential for ensuring better quality and more integrated services. For children with DCD, professionals are required to evaluate the way they collaborate, commission and deliver children's services to the optimum benefit. In some local authorities multi-agency assessments are now taking place, with joint training for health and education staff as well as joined-up strategies for intervention. As part of the training for achieving standards outlined in the NSF, exemplar materials are now available and include a series of 'patients' journeys (see the DfES TeacherNet website: Teachernet.gov.uk). The idea is that they provide a benchmark for multi-agency working, giving practical examples of how joined-up working can be achieved effectively. In line with this thinking, transdisciplinary models of working are considered in Chapter 8. This involves sharing or transferring information and skills across traditional disciplinary boundaries to enable one or two team members to be the primary workers supported by others working as consultants. Thus an occupational therapist, for example, working in the traditional, more front-line manner, would devote more time to work in conjunction with the schools advisory service in order to support teachers and assistants. This model has the benefits of influencing more people and indirectly meeting the needs of more children given that recent research indicates that paediatric occupational health waiting lists average around 46 weeks (NAPOT, 2003).

Teacher training

Governments across the UK are committed to develop more inclusive educational systems. In England and Wales these are outlined in the statutory framework for SEN provided by the Education Act 1996 and the SENDA 2001. Further afield the United Nations Education, Scientific and Cultural Organisation (UNESCO) Salamanca Statement defines the principle of inclusive schooling as 'one which should respond to the diverse needs of students accommodating both different styles of curricular, organisational arrangements and teaching strategies' (UNESCO, 1994, p.11). This backdrop has provided us with the necessary legislative framework through which to embed good practice for children with DCD into our schools. Exemplary classroom practices now need to reflect quantitative and qualitative data demonstrating pupil achievement that has been suggested throughout this book.

If, as Thomas (1997) predicts, the third millennium is witness to significant changes in the practice of including all pupils in their local school, it would appear that inclusion will continue to increase. The challenge in education lies in enabling classroom practitioners to identify children with DCD, to gather baseline and assessment information and then be able to put in place an appropriate curriculum that will cater for their needs. The chapters that follow are designed to help teachers consider and reflect on ways in which they can enhance their own individual pedagogy. This process can be carried out in conjunction with meeting targets as part of a teacher's continuous professional development rolling programme. The overall effects of developing the skills and knowledge of the classroom practitioner are the inevitable consequences of increasing the opportunities for all learners, including those with DCD.

Listening to the voice of the child

One area of the Code of Practice which has received less attention is that of the pupil's own direct involvement in the assessment and learning process, in particular considering pupils' views in identifying their difficulties, setting goals and agreeing a developmental strategy (SENCOP 2001). The final two chapters of this book are devoted to accounts drawn from parents as well as the children themselves who have coordination difficulties. Without a doubt, no amount of careful planning and research or carefully designed models of intervention can really be effective if we are not listening to those young people who have first-hand experience. Their accounts help to provide the reader with empathy for their plight and in doing so provide curriculum coordinators with the anecdotal evidence that will help shape the educational environment that these children are expected to participate in.

This book is ultimately about how we can provide better scaffolding and support systems for pupils with DCD and make the reasonable adjustments necessary for them to access the curriculum. There is still much work to do but the commitment of professionals, parents and children to find solutions together is at the heart of school improvement, an establishment which seeks to unlock the true potential for all of our future generation.

Specific Learning Difficulties: The Spectrum

Gavin Reid

This chapter will provide an overview of the range of conditions and characteristics that can be associated with specific learning difficulties (SpLD). It is important to recognize that SpLD can be seen as a spectrum of overlapping difficulties, and most of the syndromes associated with SpLD describe a cluster of difficulties and discrepancies experienced by children.

The purpose of this chapter is therefore to:

■ describe some issues relating to the overlapping characteristics within the spectrum of specific learning difficulties;

■ discuss the research background in relation to the overlap, or co-association between these difficulties; and

■ provide insights into how these syndromes and their specific characteristics can become meaningful for the teacher in terms of identification criteria and intervention programmes and strategies.

There will be particular reference to developmental coordination disorders (DCD) throughout this chapter.

Labels and overlap – issues and concerns

There are a number of issues relating to the use of labels to describe particular specific learning difficulties. These issues include:

■ the confusion relating to the overlap between the characteristics of individual specific difficulties;

■ the criteria used for the identification of specific conditions; and

■ the most appropriate type of intervention and provision.

It might in fact be suggested that it is more useful to focus on the actual characteristics rather than the conditions, and particularly how these characteristics relate to the barriers to learning for that child. The overlap between many of the characteristics usually associated with different SpLDs can be confusing for both teachers and parents. At the same time, however, a label can result in additional resources and more appropriate support being provided. Additionally a label or a 'working definition' can bring a degree of understanding of the nature of the difficulty and this can be beneficial to all, including the child.

Some terms or labels, however, used to describe specific learning difficulties are not well defined and can be vague, controversial and misleading. Even labels that are commonly used such as dyslexia, dyspraxia, dyscalculia, dysgraphia, ADHD (attention deficit hyperactivity disorder), DCD (developmental coordination disorders) and Tourette syndrome, as well as language and social disorders such as autism and Asperger's syndrome, can all be misleading and are not always easy to define and diagnose. Many of these are the subject of ongoing controversy and different theoretical positions are evident (see BPS, 1999, regarding dyslexia and Lloyd and Norris, 1999, regarding ADHD). Although labels are commonly used for the above conditions the diagnosis can still be far from precise. Often a diagnosis emerges from clinical judgement that is based on evidence from checklists or screening tests. The diagnosis can be further compounded by the overlapping characteristics. DCD is a case in point as the characteristics associated with DCD can often overlap with other conditions such as literacy difficulties, attention difficulties, language difficulties and dysgraphia. In this situation it may be difficult to identify the principal difficulty(ies) experienced by the child.

According to the classification in DSM IV (American Psychiatric Association, 1994), developmental coordination disorders (DCD) are recognised by a marked impairment in the development of motor coordination, particularly if this impairment significantly interferes with academic achievement or activities of daily life. Portwood (2004) indicates how the manifestations of DCD can vary with age and development. It is also important to recognize the key phrases in the criteria for DSM–IV: 'marked impairment' and 'significantly interferes'. These phrases indicate that some children may show some of the characteristics of DCD, but if they do not meet the criteria relating to 'marked impairment that significantly interferes with progress' then there may be a case for the category not being applied. There are, however, a number of children who will show some of the factors relating to DCD but these may not be sufficient for a diagnosis. These children may, however, have a range of other difficulties that can be associated with other types of specific learning difficulties.

It may therefore be more useful for the teacher to be aware of the specific characteristics of an individual child's profile. This also highlights the view that children can have different profiles for the same difficulty. For example, some children with characteristics of DCD may also have significant difficulties in working memory, while other children may not.

Characteristics, as opposed to labels, can take on a more descriptive role. Characteristics for a number of specific learning difficulties can include to a greater or lesser extent aspects relating to:

- working memory deficits;

- auditory processing;

- fine motor difficulties;

- phonological difficulties;

- non-verbal difficulties; and

- literacy difficulties.

One of the principal areas of confusion therefore in the use of labels is the overlap that exists between different syndromes.

Spectrum of difficulties

The broad range of the difficulties associated with the term specific learning difficulties can be subdivided into the following categories:

- language-related difficulties;

- attention difficulties;

- motor difficulties;

- social difficulties.

It has been noted, however, that some children may possess characteristics that fall into each of these above categories (Weedon and Reid, 2003). Weedon and Reid point out that children who present with the same range of difficulties in the classroom situation and may have the same label can have underlying needs that are very different and therefore will need different responses from the school. This emphasizes the view that all specific learning difficulties should be placed within a continuum. This continuum can range from mild to severe and there will be individual variations. This means that not all children within the same category will necessarily exhibit the same specific cluster of difficulties (see Fig. 2.1) to the same degree. At the same time it also highlights the view that intervention should be contextualized to the individual and not to the category or label (see Fig. 2.2).

In Figure 2.1 four areas of difficulties are highlighted: language-related difficulties, movement and motor difficulties, attention difficulties and social difficulties. Children with DCD and other specific difficulties can show difficulties in each of these areas but almost certainly not to the same degree. A child therefore can be very high in the continuum of severity for movement and attention difficulties but low in social and language difficulties. This and the continuum of needs shown in Figure 2.2 highlight the need to view children with specific learning difficulties in an individual way. For example, in Figure 2.2, if a child is low in social skills then he/she will require maximum exposure in social tasks such as group work but may not require maximum exposure in print skills.

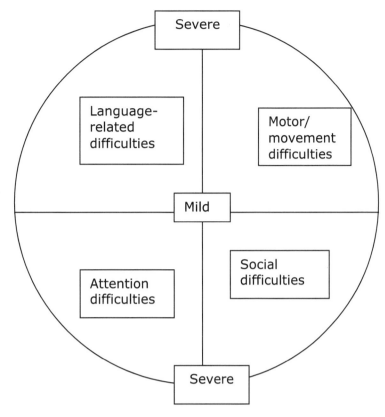

Figure 2.1 Development coordination disorder (DCD) continuum of difficulties.

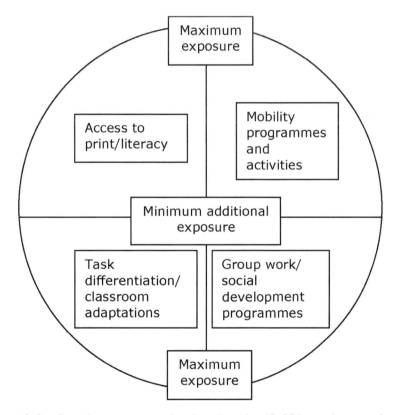

Figure 2.2 Development coordination disorder (DCD) continuum of needs.

The use of labels and the role of definitions

A label can have different meanings to different people. There is often a lack of consensus about precise definitions in most of the known specific learning difficulties. The same words and labels may be used in quite different ways, by different professionals. For example, the judgement one has to make on what is a 'significant' or 'marked' difficulty can differ. There can be questions relating to exactly what constitutes a 'discrepancy'. For example, does DCD relate to a discrepancy between 'apparent' academic potential and current levels of attainment in motor tasks? It may in fact be more useful to describe DCD as a cluster of characteristic features, regardless of intellectual potential or level of attainments, that can relate to impaired motor/perceptual/organizational skills.

It is important that the teacher has a sound understanding of the underlying characteristics and the factors that underpin a specific condition. In relation to dyslexia Reason (2002) suggests that an operational definition should be developed and utilized by education authorities. This implies that any definition is really meaningless unless it can be operationalized and understood within the classroom context. This can apply to virtually all known specific learning difficulties. The situation regarding definitions can be made more complex for the class teacher when one considers the influence of different professional groups. Taking ADHD as an example, Lloyd and Norris (1999) have suggested there are three main streams of influence: medical, educational and social. Each of these groups can have different definitions of ADHD and different priorities in relation to assessment and intervention.

Professional perspectives

As indicated above, the difficulties of diagnosis and intervention can be compounded by the range of different professionals who may be involved with a child with SpLD. Portwood (2000) speaks of '... the difficulties and frustrations experienced by children and their families who move between professionals in an attempt to obtain a diagnosis'. It can be suggested that even the most rigorously derived label for a specific learning difficulty may be no more than a general description of the difficulty.

Fawcett and Nicolson (2004) highlight the overlapping neurological connections involved in information processing, particularly relating to print, which have been encapsulated in the cerebellum deficit hypothesis. In this theoretical position Fawcett and Nicolson show how motor factors can be implicated with phonological processing and visual processing through the connecting processing mechanisms involving the cerebellum. Using this hypothesis it is not surprising that many children with specific learning difficulties showing language/perceptual and motor difficluties have common elements and clear areas of overlap.

In fact Biedermanet et al. (1990) show how research evidence indicates that more than 50 per cent of children with a diagnosis of DCD meet the requirements of at least two disorders. Ramus, Pidgeon and Frith (2003) suggest that many children with dyslexia show an overlap with ADHD and DCD, while Kaplan et al. (1998) reported that 63 per cent of the sample they studied also had DCD.

This situation is made more complex by the lack of clear criteria for diagnosis. This is in fact the situation with most of the known SpLDs, including DCD. Portwood (2004) reports on the study by Geuze et al. (2001) who reviewed 164 publications on the study of DCD and found that only 60 per cent were based on objective criteria. Furthermore, Missiuna (1996) suggests that although there are some criteria for the identification of DCD, such as impaired motor skills and the absence of physical and intellectual disorders, they are certainly not a homogeneous group. It seems therefore that even within an umbrella term like specific learning difficulties there are subsets of umbrella terms and DCD can be considered to be one of those subsets. Ripley (2001) suggests that DCD is the term that is used in the guidelines for DSM IV because DSM IV includes reference to key elements in DCD such as information processing, conceptualizing and planning motor output and sensory integration.

It is important therefore to acknowledge the range of difficulties within DCD and within the more generic umbrella term SpLD. This has implications for a clear understanding of the characteristics of DCD and particularly for the criteria for assessment. It also has implications for the use of a label, an issue that is discussed later in this chapter. McIntyre and Deponio (2003) discuss the advantages and disadvantages of using labels and recognise that a label can help to access resources, provide a description of the difficulty, bring relief to both children and parents and help to identify the most appropriate strategies. At the same time they recognize that a label can be limiting and misleading and for some children may even be distressing as they may 'resent any suggestion that they should meet other children just like them' (p. 36).

Identification and assessment

The model put forward by Morton and Frith (1995) – the causal modelling framework – provides a comprehensive framework for understanding the different factors and variables that can contribute to specific learning difficulties. This can have implications for assessment as the framework (see Fig. 2.3) incorporates cognitive and classroom perspectives as well as environmental influences. The identification of the difficulties relating to SpLD therefore must be comprehensive and precise, but they should also be task- and classroom-related. Developmental factors such as the child's current level of development and attainment, as well the task, need to be considered.

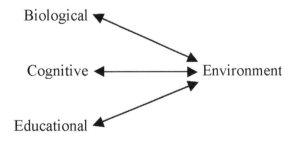

Figure 2.3 Causal modelling framework.

(Adapted from Frith, 2002.)

13

It can be suggested that specific learning difficulties do not often occur in isolation. Overlap is in fact the norm rather than the exception. Rasmussen and Gillberg (2000) comment that the most common practice seems to be to diagnose only one syndrome. For instance, if a 10-year-old boy has a combination of multiple motor and vocal tics, pervasive attention-deficit problems and dyslexia, it is quite common to diagnose only Tourette syndrome, even though a case could be made for diagnosing ADHD and dyslexia also. This failure of diagnosis, Ramussen and Gillberg suggest, should become less of a problem once there is a general acceptance that co-morbidity is common and in fact perhaps the rule.

There has been increasing interest in identification criteria for the different specific learning difficulties and a number of instruments have been developed to identify many of these, for example Conners (1996) for ADHD, Fawcett and Nicolson (1996) for the dyslexia screening test, Portwood (1999) for dyspraxia and Henderson, Came and Brough (2003) for dyscalculia. While these have considerable merit it is important to ensure a constant focus on the learning environment and the learning experiences of the child. It important to access the wider picture and incorporate aspects of the learning environment into the assessment process. This implies that assessment involves more than utilizing a test but in fact refers to a process, and that process involves more than administering a test. It involves observing the child in a range of learning contexts and undertaking different tasks over a period of time. Additionally, it also involves obtaining information from teacher observations as well as from parents.

A possible generic diagnostic framework for the assessment of specific learning difficulties could cover the following aspects:

- sensory assessment;
- family information;
- classroom behaviours;
- attention levels;
- attainment levels;
- comprehension test;
- free writing;
- curriculum information;
- observational assessment in different learning contexts using a contextualized schedule to ensure that a range of activities are covered in the assessment;
- additional relevant information.

Weedon and Reid have sought to deal with the overlap by developing a profiling system of assessment and intervention (Weedon and Reid, 2003). This involves the use of descriptive criteria for 17 major conditions that are associated with the most commonly known specific learning difficulties detailed in a computer-aided instrument called SNAP (Special Needs Assessment Profile).

Overcoming barriers to learning

Although many children with DCD may also share some characteristics with children diagnosed as having ADHD, dyslexia or language-delay, the intervention priorities can actually be different. For example, the child with DCD may have good literacy skills but have difficulty in both attention and coordination, therefore the needs of that particular child will be different from a typical child with dyslexia who may have major difficulties in accessing print.

It is crucial therefore that the specific characteristics – and how these characteristics may provide a barrier to the child completing a specific task within the curriculum – are identified. This means that the task, curriculum and environmental considerations will be key elements in an intervention programme.

Concluding comments

This chapter has sought to demonstrate that while it is important to have a clear picture of the specific characteristics that contribute to a label such as DCD it is also important to recognize the needs and the differences in each child and to reflect these in learning and teaching programmes. The overlap between specific difficulties is common and the norm rather than the exception. This can be confusing and at times convey contradictory messages to the class teacher. It is crucial therefore that the different conditions that represent the spectrum of specific learning difficulties are understood and clearly defined. Given the controversy and uncertainty that surrounds the identification criteria it might also be useful to focus on the presenting characteristics of the specific learning difficulty. This would imply that the key aspect is to identify the barriers that prevent curriculum access. Irrespective of the approach adopted in the conceptual understanding, the identification and the intervention of DCD and the other specific learning difficulties, it is important to adopt a bigger picture and view the child and the learning environment in a holistic and global manner.

Developing Service Provision in Schools

Nichola Jones

Why LEAs and schools need to consider provision

When children have difficulty performing everyday motor tasks, the problem can impact on their self-esteem, on how they interact with other children as well as on their behaviour and academic performance. Helping children with these difficulties access the curriculum as early as possible can prevent the development of secondary problems including low self-esteem and behavioural difficulties.

What needs to be in place?

Local education authorities (LEAs) and schools need to consider a framework they can put in place to develop local provision (see Fig. 3.1). In the first instance raising awareness of the difficulties youngsters with poor coordination may have will need to be considered. This could be done through school INSET. Identification and assessment procedures will need to be incorporated into the school development plan and special needs policy. Ways of adapting the curriculum as well as intervention programmes need to be developed alongside small-scale teacher research projects that identify proven and successful strategies.

Where to start

This chapter provides some examples that can be used by LEAs and schools to help children with DCD and also those children who have poor coordination. Examples of checklists that can be administered by teachers to collect baseline information are shown. Specialist staff, including advisory SEN and PE teachers, may want to consider specific tests that can be used to collect qualitative and quantitative data in relation to motor skills. The use of this sort of data aids in the measurement of targets within the classroom as well as providing criteria for the allocation of additional resources. The enhancement of teacher skills to deliver a suitably adapted curriculum can be achieved through professional development programmes.

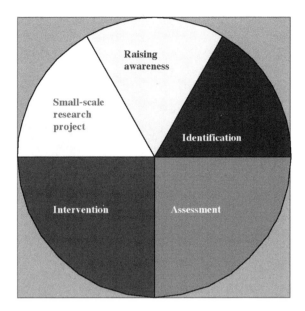

Figure 3.1 A framework for developing school provision.

This chapter also provides suggestions that promote accessibility in order to enhance services for children with coordination difficulties.

The sections include:

- the identification of children with coordination difficulties

- teacher assessment

- the role of the outside specialist

- resources

- further reading

The identification of children with coordination difficulties

When children start school the teacher will be aware of the progress they are making towards developmental goals through the collection of baseline data as well as classroom observation. It may be that areas of difficulty such as handwriting or physical education trigger concern by the class teacher for children with coordination difficulties.

It is early diagnosis and appropriate intervention that can improve the prospects of children with special educational needs. This can reduce the need for expensive intervention later on.

What to do if the school has a concern

Within the guidelines set out in the SEN Code of Practice (2001) the trigger for school action is where the teacher expresses concern that a child is showing signs of having difficulty with coordination and associated activities despite receiving differentiated learning opportunities.

Teacher checklists

A teacher checklist is a history of past and present behaviours in order to identify areas where children are having difficulty in the educational setting. The separate checklists that are presented here have been created for primary and secondary school children by Bridgend County Borough Council. The forms require teachers to indicate characteristics displayed by the child and can be helpful in setting goals and targets. The checklists can be used to provide the school and outside agencies with some indication of the specific areas of difficulties for pupils.

Developmental coordination disorder
The primary school pupil

Name of pupil: _____

School: _____

Date of birth: _____ Class teacher: _____

Recent SATs results: _____

Reading/Spelling/Maths test scores: _____

Is the pupil:

- Following an IEP   Yes ☐   No ☐

- Receiving extra support in class   Yes ☐   No ☐
  (non-teaching)

- Withdrawn for lessons   Yes ☐   No ☐

- In a special class/unit   Yes ☐   No ☐

Motor development

Appears un-coordinated ☐

Poor naming and locating of body parts ☐

Trouble judging the force needed to throw balls ☐

Lack of control and direction when throwing a ball ☐

Poor balance, both static and dynamic ☐

Poor posture and muscle tone ☐

Uses either foot to kick ☐

Problems with running and jumping ☐

Difficulty with buttons, laces and fine motor skills when dressing ☐

Poor left and right awareness, including poorly established hand preference ☐

Poor memory of past instructions involving motor skills ☐

Midline problems causing lack of coordination between the two sides of the body ☐

Cannot use the two hands together for skills ☐

Has no awareness of up and down, before and behind ☐

Poor awareness of space ☐

Handwriting and scissor skills

Unable to sit appropriately on a chair when writing ☐

Poor pencil grip ☐

Applies too much/little pressure on pencil ☐

Poor handwriting letter formation ☐

Poor spacing between words ☐

The writing includes an incorrect mixture of upper and lower case lettering ☐

Difficulty with numbers and geometric shapes ☐

No distinction between ascenders (bdhkt) and descenders (gjpy) ☐

Slow speed of writing ☐

Difficulty with practical tasks like using scissors ☐

Motor organization

Difficulty with the order of garments when dressing ☐

Difficulty organizing work, loses and drops things, forgets the right school books, leaves homework at home, also has difficulty organizing time ☐

Cannot tell directions, gets lost easily – may have difficulty finding way around the school ☐

Visual perception

Poor planning and layout of work ☐

Spacing of words and the size of the letters varies from day to day ☐

Difficulty remembering an image when it is removed, for example copying from the board ☐

Poor visual sequential memory – remembering a series of visual images in order ☐

Auditory perception

Difficulty in discriminating appropriate sounds in the classroom, e.g. teacher's/children's voices in the classroom ☐

Difficulty discriminating and focusing on appropriate sounds and ignoring background noise ☐

Difficulty recalling sounds in order including following directions, completing a sentence in order: 'the ball is blue' and not 'ball blue is' ☐

Comments:

_____

_____

_____

_____

_____

_____

_____

_____

_____

_____

_____

_____

_____

_____

_____

_____

_____

_____

_____

Name: _____

Designation: _____

Date: _____

Developmental coordination disorder
The secondary school pupil

Name of pupil: _____

School: _____

Date of birth: _____ Class teacher: _____

Special needs coordinator: _____

Most recent SATs results: _____

Is the pupil:

■ Following an IEP   Yes ☐   No ☐
(please attach a copy to the questionnaire)

■ Receiving extra support in class   Yes ☐   No ☐
(non-teaching)?

■ Withdrawn for lessons?   Yes ☐   No ☐

■ In a special class/unit?   Yes ☐   No ☐

Appears clumsy or poorly coordinated ☐

Has difficulty manipulating own body and other objects in space ☐

Has poor posture when sitting which may deteriorate during the day ☐

Has difficulty with handwriting – Poor letter formation ☐

Poorly spaced letters ☐

Cannot stay on lines ☐

Excessive pressure used ☐

Has difficulty spacing work for diagrams and pictures ☐

Has difficulty with taking dictation or recalling detailed instruction ☐

Has difficulty copying from the whiteboard ☐

Has difficulty using equipment in the classroom – rulers, scissors, compass ☐

Is disorganised and has difficulties following a timetable, finding his/her
way around school building ☐

Has difficulty reading (the size and print may be an issue, as well as the volume of print on the page and the starkness in contrast between the white page and black print) ☐

Spills or knocks things over excessively ☐

Has difficulty in PE ☐

Has difficulty changing for PE/games ☐

Comments:

_____

_____

_____

_____

_____

_____

_____

_____

_____

_____

_____

_____

_____

_____

_____

Name: _____

Designation: _____

Date: _____

...ecklist

	Yes	Consider
...nsure which hand to hold the pencil in?		Hand dominance
...n abnormal grip?		Grip
Does the child sit appropriately on a chair when writing?		Posture
Does the child slump forward onto the table when writing?		Posture
Does the child position the paper awkwardly when writing?		Paper position
Does the child lift their wrist off the paper when writing?		Grip
Is too much pressure applied through the pencil?		Grip
Is too little pressure applied through the pencil?		Grip
Are letters formed appropriately?		Letter formation
Are reversed or inverted letters evident?		Letter formation
Does the child commence writing at the left side of the page?		Left to right
Does the writing slope downwards across a page rather than follow a horizontal direction?		Letter formation
Are inadequate spaces left between words?		Spacing
Are the sizes of letters erratic?		Size of letters
Are letters incompletely formed, i.e. the cross bar is missing from the 't'?		Letter formation
Does the child's writing contain an erratic mixture of upper and lower case lettering?		Letter formation
Do you struggle to identify distinct ascenders and descenders in the child's writing?		Size of letters

▶

Observations	Yes	Consider
Does the child struggle to join letters appropriately?		Joins
Does writing appear slow and laboured?		Speed
Is the speed of writing slow?		Speed

This form can be photcopied. © *Developing School Provision for Children with Dyspraxia* 2005.

Handwriting speed and legibility test

In order to collect the information listed on the handwriting checklist the following legibility and speed test could be administered.

Equipment

- Legibility and speed sheets
- Pen/pencil
- Stopwatch

The test

When testing an individual the activity should be timed. The duration of the test is three minutes. The pupil from the junior sector is asked to copy the sentence 'The quick brown fox jumps over the lazy dog'. Pupils from the infants sector copy the words 'cats and dogs'. This should be done:

- as quickly as possible;
- without correcting;
- as neatly as possible.

Results

The following copying speeds have been compiled from Alton (1992) and Ziviani and Watson-Will (1998).

Norms for handwriting speed suggest that:

A child of 7 years writes	28 letters a minute
8	36
9	45
10	52
11	60
12	67
13	75 letters or 13–15 words
	100 letters or 20 words a minute

Handwriting legibility and speed test (Junior)

The quick brown fox jumps over the lazy dog

_____

_____

_____

_____

_____

_____

_____

_____

_____

Handwriting legibility and speed test (Infant)

Cats and dogs

_____

_____

_____

_____

_____

_____

_____

Everyday living skills checklist

Observations (Can the child...)	Yes/ No	Comments
Manage the toilet without help?		
Wash hands adequately after messy activities?		
Dress/undress at the same speed as the others in the group?		
Put on clothing in the correct order and orientation with a tidy(ish) result?		
Manage fastening such as Velcro, large buttons, zips?		
Keep track of personal possessions?		
Collect the materials needed for a task with minimal help?		

▶

Observations (Can the child...)	Yes/ No	Comments
Move around the classroom without falling or bumping into children and furniture?		
Navigate around the school?		
Use knife and fork neatly, cut own meat?		
Tie shoe laces?		
Is the child particularly accident-prone in the playground?		

This form can be photocopied. © *Developing School Provision for Children with Dyspraxia* 2005.

Comments: _____

_____

_____

_____

_____

_____

_____

_____

_____

_____

Date: _____

Dressing and undressing checklist

Observations *(Can the child...)*	Yes/ No	Comments
Take off socks?		
Put on socks?		
Take off T-shirt/sweatshirt?		
Put on T-shirt/sweatshirt?		
Take off trousers or skirt with elasticated waistband?		
Put on trousers or skirt with elasticated waistband?		
Unfasten and fasten buttons?		
Tie laces?		
Open and close zips (closed end)?		
Open and close zips (open end)?		
Put on clothing in the right order?		

This form can be photocopied. © *Developing School Provision for Children with Dyspraxia* 2005.

Comments: _____

_____

_____

_____

_____

Date: _____

Meal times

Observations (Can the child...)	Yes/ No	Comments
Sit still in a chair?		
Use a spoon?		
Use a fork?		
Use a knife?		
Use a knife and fork to cut food?		
Manipulate food without moving the plate?		
Eat as quickly as most of the other children?		
Handle drinks without spillage (mostly)?		
Carry a dinner tray independently?		

This form can be photocopied. © *Developing School Provision for Children with Dyspraxia* 2005.

Comments: _____

_____

_____

_____

_____

_____

_____

Date: _____

Teacher assessment

The collection of information for children with coordination difficulties is vital for providing a baseline on which to plan intervention programmes. The information also means that children's progress can be monitored using quantitative and qualitative data.

Observing pupils

Observing children while they perform tasks in the classroom, take part in physical education or play in their playground helps the teacher determine how well they function during different activities. Unstructured observation is where the observation takes place during naturally occurring events such as physical education. Here the environment is not adapted or modified.

Structured observations are when specific activities are performed at a specified time. This is a useful and important way of collecting information about a child. In particular, for children with coordination difficulties, it encourages teachers to become good observers of human movement.

Standardized tests

Standardized tests are used to look at specific skills and are administered to a group of children who are the same age. The child's score is compared with the scores received by all the others in the group. The child's performance is calculated into percentiles or standard scores. If, for example, a child's score was at the sixth percentile, it indicates that out of 100 children 94 children scored higher.

Often physiotherapists, occupational therapists and educational psychologists, as well as advisory and specialist teachers, administer standardized tests to determine the severity of children's motor delays. The information obtained from the standardized tests can be used to develop measurable goals and objectives in the school environment. This section looks at the Movement ABC standardized test for the collection of information about a child's motor dysfunction.

The Movement ABC

One of the standardized tests used by a range of professionals, including advisory teachers and specialist PE teachers, is the *Movement Assessment Battery for Children* (1992), written by Professor David Sugden and Dr Sheila Henderson and published by and available from the Psychological Corporation (ISBN 0-7491-0168-7).

The *Movement ABC* may be administered by professionals with a wide range of expertise and experience. From the education professions, psychologists, physical education teachers, teachers in special education and classroom teachers may find it helpful; from the health professions, paediatricians and physio, occupational and speech therapists may find it provides them with useful information.

To use the Test and Checklist in their standard format, no special training is required. Examiners require familiarity with the general procedures of standardized testing and some experience of working with children, especially pre-schoolers and children with special educational needs.

Using the *Movement ABC* Test with qualitative observations is more difficult and requires skill and experience in observing children. For some professionals, these skills will have been developed during their specialist training; for others, additional training may have to be sought.

The *Movement ABC* has the following features:

- It is concerned with the identification and description of impairments of motor function in children.

- The test provides objective quantitative data on performance. Its score indicates the extent to which a child falls below the level of his or her age peers. No attempt is made to differentiate between children who perform above this level. Age norms are provided for children aged 4 to 12, based upon a representative sample of over 1,200 children.

- Administration of the basic form of the test takes 20–40 minutes depending on the age and degree of difficulty experienced by the child.

- The formal assessment is paralleled by an observational approach designed to help the examiner observe how the child performs each task in the test, and to pinpoint emotional and motivational difficulties the child may have in relation to motor tasks.

- It provides a structured framework within which to identify a child's strengths and weaknesses and to indicate directions for further assessment or remediation.

- The Manual includes a complete section designed to support the management and remediation of movement difficulties.

- It may be used by professionals with a variety of backgrounds and training from both the educational and medical fields.

(Sugden and Henderson, 1992, pp. 2–3)

The test consists of four age bands:

Age Band   1   (4/5 + 6 year olds)

              2   (7 + 8 year olds)

              3   (9 + 10 year olds)

              4   (11 + 12 year olds)

The tests consist of four sections:

- manual dexterity;

- ball skills;

- static balance;

- dynamic balance.

An example of the Movement ABC manual dexterity test for age band 4, 5 and 6 years: posting coins

Materials

- Bank box

- 12 plastic coins

- Table-top mat

- Stopwatch

Set-up

Place the bank box on the table-top mat with its short side towards the child. On the side of the box corresponding to the preferred hand arrange the coins in four horizontal rows of three, with approximately one inch between columns and rows. To test the other hand, reverse the position of the bank box and coins.

Task

The child holds the box steady with one hand and grasps a coin with the other. The edge of the coin must touch the mat until the child is told to begin. At a signal, the child drops the coins through the slot in the bank box, one at a time, as quickly as possible. Stop timing when the last coin strikes the bottom of the box. Both hands are tested.

Qualitative observations

The test consists of a list of qualitative data that examiners are asked to consider when carrying out the assessment. This includes:

- Body control/posture

- Does not look at slot while inserting coins

- Holds face too close to task

- Holds head at an odd angle

- Does not use pincer grip to pick up coins

- Exaggerates finger movements in releasing coins

- Does not use the supporting hand to hold box steady

- Does *extremely* poorly with one hand

- Changes hands or uses both hands during a trial

- Hand movements are jerky

- Sitting posture is poor

- Moves constantly/fidgets

Quantitative data

Finally, the test is scored against a set of quantitative data providing an age equivalent banding:

Record time taken (secs); **F** for failure; **R** for refusal; **I** for inappropriate

Preferred hand
Trial 1 ....
Trial 2 ....

Non-preferred hand
Trial 1 ....
Trial 2 ....

Age 4	Age 5	Age 6		Score			Age 4	Age 5	Age 6
0–23	0–20	0–17		0	0		0–27	0–23	0–20
24–25	21	18–19		1	1		28–30	24–25	21–22
26–27	22	20		2	2		31–33	26	23
28–32	23–24	21–24		3	3		34–47	27	24–25
33–49	25–29	25–28		4	4		48–55	28–32	26–29
50+	30+	29+		5	5		56+	33+	30+

*Item score

*Item score = (Preferred hand + Non-preferred hand) ÷ 2

The final data provides the tester with norm referenced age equivalent score. This is particularly useful information as it informs the school about the severity of the child's impairment in relation to his/her peer group. From an LEA perspective criteria can be developed alongside quantitative data, including an age equivalent normative score, for the provision of outside agency support. This data also provides useful information for evaluating the effectiveness of intervention programmes put in place within the school context.

Developmental Test of Visual Perception

The DTVP-2 (Hammill et al., 2000) is a battery of eight subtests that measure different but interrelated visual and visual-motor abilities. The battery is designed for use with children aged between 4 and 10. It helps to establish the presence and degree of visual perceptual or visual-motor difficulties in individual children. It also helps to identify children requiring referral to other professionals or agencies. The test also helps to show the effects of special training programmes designed to help correct visual perceptual problems.

The eight subtests comprise:

- eye-hand coordination;
- position in space;
- copying;
- figure ground;
- spatial relations;
- visual closure;
- visual-motor speed;
- form constancy.

Further information can be obtained from:

The Psychological Corporation, 32 Jamestown Road, London NW1 7BY.

The role of the outside specialist

If you are concerned that a pupil is not making progress despite implementing a differentiated curriculum you should begin the process of involving the outside specialist. Advice and support may include a range of outside agencies including:

- community paediatrician;
- occupational therapist;
- physiotherapist;

- speech and language therapist;

- educational psychologist;

- advisory teacher;

- SENCo.

The role of the community paediatrician

There are a number of medical conditions that may present themselves with similarities to that of developmental coordination disorder.

The community paediatrician will investigate for signs of medical as well as neurological disease. Neurological examination will assess physical functions which include muscle tone, reflexes and range of movement.

The role of the occupational therapist

Occupational therapists will analyse the child's functional performance within different environments to identify the child's strengths and weaknesses. They determine whether limitations in performance are linked intrinsically to the child, are due to factors in the environment, or are a combination of both.

Functional performance is defined as those things that we do in everyday life, for example: dressing; grooming; washing; toileting; eating; playing; working; using tools such as scissors, pencils, cutlery, rulers. Functional performance is dependent on certain abilities, e.g. organizational skills, problem-solving skills, physical skills.

The occupational therapist is concerned with analysing the child's ability to perform in everyday contexts. Therefore referrals for an occupational therapy assessment should also indicate a problem in functional performance, e.g. the child is unable to dress himself, cannot use a knife and fork properly, cannot use a pencil appropriately.

Through assessment occupational therapists use various methods (observation, testing and interview) to determine whether components of performance are delayed, deficient or missing. The occupational therapist then considers which performance components appear to interfere with the functional abilities of the child and this forms the basis of the treatment programme, e.g. the difficulty with dressing may be due to a perceptual or fine motor problem.

The role of the physiotherapist

The role of the physiotherapist in treating the child with developmental coordination difficulties is linked very closely to the occupational therapist.

The areas a physiotherapist may assess could include postural organization, motor coordination and control, body and spatial awareness, movement sense, joint range and stability, muscle tone and strength.

The longer-term objectives of physiotherapy intervention are to gain effective body and object control, which will hopefully lead to improvement in emotional control, learning and social skills, social interactions, self-concepts and self-esteem. Improvement and development of gross motor skills can serve as a basis for more complex perceptual motor learning and the acquisition of fine motor skills, therefore close liaison with the occupational therapist in assessing and treating the child is essential.

The role of the speech and language therapist

Developmental verbal dyspraxia is a condition present from birth where the child has difficulty making and coordinating the precise movements that are used in the production of spoken language.

The child may present with some/all of the following phonological (sound) system problems:

- sound system is not following the normal development, i.e. it is not that of a younger child;

- problems with voluntary movements versus involuntary, for example the child can lick sugar from his lips when eating a bun, but not if he is asked or shown what to do;

- evidence of struggling/groping for movements – searching when trying to produce sounds;

- may be able to imitate a sound on its own but not in sequence, for example p/p/p/ or p/t/k/;

- skills deteriorate with increasing length and complexity – repeated elicited single words, short phrases, spontaneous speech sample;

- may use non-English sounds;

- inconsistent pattern of errors or variability of the same (repeated) word, for example target word 'car' may be produced 'star' or 'da' or 'car';

- vowel errors;

- difficulties in control of the prosodic features, for example intonation, lack of rhythm, nasality, voicing problems (p versus b).

The role of the speech and language therapist (SALT) is to identify the specific areas of speech and language difficulties and provide an intervention programme. These include:

- work with the SALT or SALT assistant;

- group work;

- programmes for parents/carers and school staff;

- strategies for jointly agreed targets to be included in the child's individual education plan.

37

The role of the educational psychologist

When children are referred to the educational psychologist motor skills are seldom identified as the main area of concern. Initial worries may be around behaviour, learning or physical problems. As a consequence, the educational psychologist may gather together information provided by school and parents and carry out supplementary observations and assessments, including academic attainments, assessment of visual-motor integration and handwriting, cognitive assessment and assessment of motor skills.

The role of the educational psychologist in the assessment of DCD is to work closely with parents, teachers, therapists and medical practitioners in order to:

- clarify the nature of the motor impairment;

- assess the implications for learning;

- assess the classroom as a learning environment for the child;

- assess the implications for access to the National Curriculum;

- identify the social, emotional and behavioural implication of the motor impairment.

The role of the advisory teacher

The role of the advisory teacher is to identify the strengths and weaknesses of a pupil's ability to carry out a range of gross and fine motor screening tests as well as to identify any perceptual difficulties. The purpose of the screening is to indicate areas within the class and aspects of the curriculum for which the pupil will require support and guidance.

The advisory teacher will work with the school in order to help class teachers in the delivery of the National Curriculum using a range of specialist strategies and materials.

Their role is to offer support and advice for pupils to develop gross, fine and perceptual skills within the context of the school curriculum and to offer support in developing classroom strategies for pupils with DCD. Extra attention is given to pupils during the transition periods from the infant to junior and junior to secondary phases.

The role of the SENCo

The role of the SENCo is to support class teachers in the identification of pupils with special educational needs. Where a class teacher has a concern about a pupil who is displaying some developmental coordination difficulties the provision of a screening check could be administered (see checklist earlier in chapter).

The purpose of gathering this information is to identify how pupils are functioning and the difficulties being experienced in order to ascertain their special requirements. The assessment of a pupil's special needs will lead to a description of the special provision and any resources required to meet that provision. The support activities outlined in the following sections may be included in the development of the individual education plan. The plan will highlight the nature of the support and set targets for the pupil.

If, however, after two review periods the pupil fails to make progress the SENCo may call in the outside specialists that have been described in this section for further support and guidance. In some cases children may be assessed in the context of a DCD clinic, which provides an opportunity for specialist professionals to work together to assess and plan joined up provision for children with coordination difficulties.

The developmental coordination disorder clinic

Background

The clinic comprises of a team of educational and health professionals. This includes the advisory teacher for children with coordination difficulties, the community paediatrician, an educational psychologist, a physiotherapist, an occupational therapist and a speech and language therapist.

The clinic may be held monthly depending on resources available. The clinic may take place either in an educational or health setting.

Referrals to the clinic

Applications can be made for children to be assessed at this clinic by the school doctor, educational psychologist or advisory teacher.

Applications are considered on a monthly basis at the clinic. If a child is referred to the clinic parents complete a questionnaire about the individual child. A questionnaire will also be sent to the child's class teacher in order to obtain information in the context of the school environment.

Once this information has been collated a discussion will take place at the DCD clinic. A child will either be given an appointment to attend the clinic or a decision will be made outlining an alternative route to help any difficulties a child might be having.

Assessments at the clinic

If a child is given an appointment to attend the clinic a full assessment will be carried out and may include a paediatrician, physiotherapist, occupational therapist, speech and language therapist, educational psychologist and advisory teacher.

When a child has been seen at the clinic an initial discussion of the findings will take place and a report will follow. The report will provide details of the course of action at the school and/or clinic to help the child. The progress in the educational setting is monitored by the advisory teacher.

Resources

Fact sheet for children with motor difficulties: primary school

Dale is a seven-year-old boy whose story is typical of children with DCD. He is generally clumsy inside and outside of the classroom. He has trouble dressing and undressing for PE and often appears uncoordinated during the lesson. He has poor ball skills and looks very clumsy when he runs. He often plays alone in the playground, preferring the company of younger children. He struggles with lots of tasks in the classroom including handwriting, art and craft, scissors skills and doing up his shoelaces. It takes him a long time to complete most tasks.

Identifying children with motor difficulties

What is DCD?

Developmental coordination disorder (DCD) is a condition in which there is marked impairment in the development of motor coordination, and the impairment significantly interferes with academic achievement or the activities of daily living (DSM IV, 1994). DCD may exist in isolation or may co-occur with other conditions such as dyslexia or attention deficit hyperactivity disorder (ADHD). Children with DCD usually have average or above average intellectual abilities.

What to look for

- The child may appear clumsy, awkward or uncoordinated.

- He may have difficulty in PE lessons – running, jumping, hopping, balance, ball skills, etc.

- He may not know where all his body parts are.

- He may have poor writing skills, an unusual pencil grip and be very slow carrying out written work.

- His motor skills might not match his abilities in other areas. For example, intellectual abilities in some aspects of the curriculum appear good.

- He may have difficulties with fine motor skills like using scissors and handling classroom equipment.

- Planning and layout of work may be poor as well as the ability to copy from the board.

- Dressing and undressing for PE is difficult.

- He may find following directions and sets of instructions difficult.

- He may experience secondary emotional problems such as low self-esteem and lack of motivation.

General advice and guidance for pupils with poor coordination

Difficulties	How to help
1. Poor posture (slumps forward on table or in chair).	Make sure the desk and chair are at the right height. Ensure the pupil sits squarely. Feet should be flat on the floor and the non-dominant hand should be on the desk supporting the page or book. The use of a posture pack (angle board and seat wedge) can help ensure a well supported desk position.
2. Difficulty following a set of instructions – needs to be constantly reminded to stay on task.	Break down complex sets of instructions into smaller and simpler parts. Use verbal as well as visual reminders to help complete tasks. Set up a system of checking off steps as they are accomplished. Allow extra time to complete task.
3. Bumps into classroom objects/loses concentration.	Place the child near the front of the class. They should not be placed in the main thoroughfare of traffic or near the window where they may be easily distracted. Ensure unobstructed pathway to frequently used areas like the pencil sharpener, teacher's desk.
4. Is unusually slow at completing a task; gives up easily.	Allow more time to complete an activity. Realise the amount of written work required so that the child can complete the task with his peer group. (Minimise time spent copying non-essentials, i.e. date, title of story.)
5. Difficulty changing for PE.	Allow extra time to change for PE. Suitable clothing for the child will help such as trousers with an elasticated top and ties on elastic. Pair with a buddy to help dress and undress.

▶

Difficulties	How to help
6. Difficulty in PE lessons.	Break down complex skills into smaller and simpler parts. Provide lower apparatus, brightly coloured large balls, clear simple instructions. Do not expect the child to listen and do simultaneously – they may find it difficult to listen and watch at the same time. Where possible allow the child alternatives from taking part in team games where they might be a seen as letting their side down.
7. Messy/disorganised desk/table/drawer.	Use colour coded workbooks. Timetable daily desk tidying period. Provide visual cues to ensure the right equipment for the lesson.
8a. Poor handwriting.	Trial the use of a range of triangular grips to help writing. Thick barrelled or triangular pencils can also help. Use a clipboard to hold the paper they are working on or Dycem.
8b. Difficulty learning cursive writing/written work is illegible.	Allow stories to be dictated orally to a scribe. Introduce keyboarding skills; photocopy curriculum subject questions so the child only has to write the answer. Introduce a multi-sensory handwriting programme to give additional practice.
9. Difficulty copying from the board.	Use different colours on each line. Encourage the pupil to remember two to four words at a time. If there is a lot of copying from the board provide photo-copied sheets instead.
10. Difficulty understanding the concept of time.	Use a clock or timer to promote the understanding of time. Set the period in which a task must be completed.

The Tool Box

What is the Tool Box?

The Tool Box is a collection of readily available or easily produced resources.

What is the aim of the Tool Box?

The aim of the Tool Box is to provide a range of commonly recommended equipment. The Tool Box can help teachers, learning support assistants, parents and others to build up a bank of readily available resources suitable for improving fine motor skills.

How is the Tool Box organised?

It can be organised into *three* main sections – resources for improving:

- general fine motor skills;

- handwriting;

- scissors skills.

The Tool Box builds up to provide a central reservoir of equipment to be added to, revised and amended to suit the needs of the school.

General fine motor skills
Mini-box

- Playdough

- Threading beads

- Clothes pegs

- Pegs/peg boards

- Lacing cards

- Pipe cleaners

Maxi-box

- Playdough

- Threading beads

- Clothes pegs – different strengths and sizes

- Pegs/peg boards – variety of sizes

- Lacing cards – letters/numerals/shoe shapes, etc.

- Pipe cleaners – variety of size/texture/ colour

- Button/zips – practice waistcoats/ dressing dolls

- Stress balls – variety of sizes/shapes

- Stamps and ink pads

- Turkey baster

- Handheld mazes

- Wikki Stix

▶

General fine motor skills continued

Maxi-box

- Playdough tools
- Laminated coloured pictures/mats
- Sponges
- Commercially produced games, e.g. Connect 4, Etch-a-Sketch
- Stencils

Handwriting

Mini-box

- Handhugger pens/pencils
- Chunky crayons/coloured pencils
- Ultra-pencil grips
- Ridged comfort grips
- Ridged ruler
- Selection of raised lined paper
- Plastic lower case letters
- Left-handed ruler
- Write-well mat
- Dycem/Dycem mats
- Angle board

- Write-well mat
- Dycem/Dycem mats
- Angle board
- Handwriting whiteboard
- Handwriting demonstration sheet
- Copy cat handwriting practice sheets
- Eye-hand integrated cards
- Tracing/colouring books/mazes
- Selection of pencil grips:
  - Tri-glo grip
  - Comfort grip
  - Stubbi grip
  - Triangular grip
  - Ultra grip

Maxi-box

- Chunky crayons/coloured pencils
- Ridged comfort grips
- Ridged ruler
- Selection of raised lined paper
- Plastic lower case letters
- Left-handed ruler
- Selection of pencils:
  - Handhugger pencils
  - Faber Castell – chunky versions
  - Resin pencils – Evolution pencil
  - Staedtler: Triplus – Learner's pencil

- Triangular pencils – DES
  - Staedtler – Maxi pencil
- Selection of pens:
  - Berol Handhugger pens
  - S'Move easy pens – Stabilo
- S'Move pen – Stabilo
- Yoropen
- Manuscript handwriting pen
- Ergonomix
- Lamy pen

Scissor skills

Mini-box

- Standard school scissors (right and left handed)
- Long-loop scissors (right and left handed)
- Peta – scissor skills book
- Selection of card of varying thickness
- Sugar paper

Maxi-box

- Standard school scissors (right and left handed)

- Long-loop scissors (right and left handed)
- Peta – scissor skills book
- Selection of card of varying thicknesses
- Sugar paper
- Long loop spring-loaded scissors
- Squeezy scissors (large and small)
- 'Start Cutting' book

Table 3.1 provides sources of recommended equipment.

Table 3.1 Sources of recommended equipment

Equipment	Suppliers
Angle boards	Back in Action, LDA, Philip & Tacey
Peta – 2 scissor skills book	Taskmaster
Dycem products	Consortium, Nottingham Rehab Supplies, Ways & Means
Eye-hand integrated cards	Taskmaster
Finger grip rulers	Formative Fun, LDA, NRS, W.H. Smith, Woolworths
Hand exercisers	NRS
Handwriting demonstration sheet	Taskmaster
Handwriting whiteboard	Autopress Education
Lacing cards	LDA, NES Arnold
Left-handed equipment	Consortium, Formative Fun, LDA, Left n'Write, Philip & Tacey, Taskmaster
Magnetic, wooden, plastic letters	LDA, NES Arnold, Taskmaster
Manuscript handwriting pen	Manuscript Pen Company
Non-slip writing mat	Philip & Tacey, Ways & Means, Consortium
Pencil grips	Consortium, Formative Fun, LDA, Philip & Tacey, Taskmaster
Raised line paper	Taskmaster
Scissors	Early Learning Centre, LDA, NES Arnold, NRS, Taskmaster
Seat wedge	Back in Action, NRS

Equipment	Suppliers
S'move easy pen	Formative Fun, Consortium, Philip & Tacey
Speed-up	LDA
Spring laces	NRS
'Start Cutting' book	Easy learn
Triangular pens	Consortium, County Borough Supplies, NES Arnold, LDA, Philip & Tacey
Write-well mats	Formative Fun
Yoropen	W.H. Smith, Left-hand Education

Handwriting schemes

There are many handwriting schemes to choose from on the market. A review of currently available publications can be obtained from the National Handwriting Association (see Chapter 6). This publication helps readers to provide the best scheme for their needs by giving a structured analysis of a wide range of published handwriting schemes available in the UK. Local education authorities may wish to highlight examples of good practice, where schools can visit to observe a scheme being used.

Three examples of handwriting schemes are described below.

Write Dance by Ragnhild Oussoren Voors

This scheme is a progressive music and movement programme for the development of pre-writing and writing skills in children. It uses drawing, music rhymes, rhythm and games to link up body movements with small hand finger movements.

To purchase the scheme contact Lucky Duck Publishing Ltd: ISBN 1-873942-03-6.

Write from the Start by Lois Addy and Ion Teodorescu

This publication helps develop fine motor and perceptual skills by providing structured activities that develop the muscles of the hand alongside perceptual skills required to orientate and organize letters and words.

To purchase the scheme contact LDA, Reference LL01074.

Speed Up by Lois Addy

This programme is designed for children aged 8–13 whose handwriting is slow, illegible or lacking in fluency. It includes a baseline assessment, photocopiable instruction sheets for eight weekly sessions, and advice on identifying underlying causes of difficulty and how to tackle them.

To purchase the scheme contact LDA, Reference LL01613.

Gross motor programmes: outreach support

Part of the goal of a school's physical education programme is to produce a child who is physically active and will later develop into a physically aware adult. Children with poor coordination may find it difficult participating in some aspects of PE.

A gross motor programme can help to give these children additional support to enable them to access the PE curriculum, and to improve their self-esteem and coordination in other areas of the curriculum. Pupils can be referred by the school doctor, occupational therapist, physiotherapist, SENCo or class teacher. The children selected might have poor motor skills including handwriting difficulties and may also have low self-esteem.

How many children are included and how often?

The motor programme will include up to eight children. These take place four to five times a week and for approximately 20 minutes per session. The children are collected from the classroom and change into their PE clothes in the hall. There is a short warm-up activity before the children begin the activities and a cooling down period at the end of the session.

Who carries out the programme?

The programme is administered by school staff, either by specially trained PE teachers or by support staff under the direction of the teacher. These staff have attended a training course run by the SEN Advisory Service for setting up a gross motor programme.

Getting started

Schools will be provided with a 'Gross Motor Starter Pack' outlining some of the steps to take prior to the commencement of school motor programmes. The pack also contains baseline assessment materials and a selection of programmes that can be administered around the themes of balance, travelling, ball skills and body awareness. It is recommended that schools purchase basic equipment to get the programmes started (see Figure 3.2).

Games Development Kit

Designed specifically for schools the kit assists in motor skills development, hand eye co-ordination, behavioural management. An essential kit for any group activity. Available directly from
County Borough Supplies
01656 664521

Contents

4 Mini Playballs	20 70mm Playballs
4 Centraplay Rackets	25 Flexi Markers
4 Plastic Playbats	4 Bean Bags
4 Fun Rings	4 36cm Flat Hoops
2 Maxiplay Balls	1 Foam Dice
10 Plastic Skipping Ropes	
2 Plastic Table Tennis Bats	
4 63mm Perforated Play Balls	
Supplied in a Vinyl Holdall	Order Code D4571

Figure 3.2 Gross motor skills – Motor Programme Starter Pack

School support

Children are assessed on balance, ball skills and manual dexterity before and after participating in the eight-week programme. The results are collated by the LEA as part of its monitoring and evaluation programme. Recommendations for further intervention by the advisory service are given where appropriate.

Three schools in the district also hold demonstration lessons, which are run by specialist PE staff. An outreach PE teacher also provides support for schools to help set up and run the programme.

For further information about developing a motor programme see Chapter 6.

Assessing Pupils with Coordination Difficulties

Barbara Walsh

Introduction

Assessment is a process that gives both the pupil and the teacher an insight into learning. Learning is associated with a permanent change in the behaviour of the learner. To make sure learning has taken place, it must be assessed to see if the learning outcomes have been achieved. It is this process that helps to provide a constructive foundation for future planning and target setting as well as supplying the teacher with a valuable insight into the success of their own teaching and planning, including highlighting effective and ineffective aspects. This chapter aims to examine the importance of assessment in the learning of new skills and how this information can be used to progress learning. It is important to make sure that every child, regardless of their ability, is working to their full potential. As movement is very often assessed in physical education many of the examples will be drawn from this setting.

When do you assess?

Assessment, according to Capel (2001: 287), 'covers all the activities undertaken by teachers and others to measure the effectiveness of teaching and learning.' Assessment takes place for many reasons, perhaps in order to select or assign pupils, as an indicator of how well a task or concept is understood, to motivate pupils, to monitor progress, or more generally to give feedback to both teacher, pupil and parents.

Since we live in an information society, where we are always collecting, analysing, storing and retrieving data, it is important to determine the information that will be meaningful to the pupil and teacher rather than just fulfilling the school policy. Frapwell, Glass and Pearce (2002, p. 24) stated: 'To view assessment as divorced from the planning, teaching and learning process results in the implementation of a meaningless bolt on model, a bureaucratic monster or a task to satisfy senior management requirements.'

If assessment is to play an important part in teaching and learning and not simply act as a 'bolt on' it has to happen all the time in every situation. This is known as formative assessment, which means it is ongoing. For children with development coordination disorder (DCD) little and often is a phrase often used. This means practising skills every day for 20 minutes rather than a 45-minute block twice a week. It is easier to keep the child motivated for a short period of time and it also becomes part of their daily routine. The ongoing assessment of these tasks will help the teacher build up a comprehensive profile of the child. Thus a teacher needs to identify a pupil's movement concepts and motor skills – what the body does, where the body moves, how the body moves and with whom or with what the body moves. It is vital that these basic movement patterns are established for children with poor coordination in order to move onto more specialist skills. A child might have good control when using small movements, but large motor movements prove more difficult, as in catching or kicking a ball. The assessment strategy needs to identify these children so frustration and failure do not set in.

What is it you are going to assess?

In young children movement patterns are important in walking, throwing a ball and jumping in the air. They are movement patterns with a definitive arrangement of muscle actions which are achieved to fulfil the desired outcome. However, assessment is not just about observing movement patterns and motor abilities, but is an integrated process that builds up a picture of the whole child. Much of this work on movement, which has been influenced by Laban's framework (cited in Hodgson, 1990) not only considers movement to be of prime importance in the shaping of attitudes and relationships but a vital force in education. Bailey (1999) comments, 'there is little doubting the central importance of movement and physical activity in the lives of children and young people.' In his research he found physical play as the first appearing and most frequently occurring expression in infants and physical competence as a major factor influencing social acceptance in children of all ages and both sexes. There is a need therefore to build up a picture of strengths and weaknesses, not just of motor skills but how this affects the child emotionally and whether self-concept is affected. Is the lack of motor skills affecting other areas of learning? Is it affecting the child's interaction with other children? Is it making them unhappy? Are any other behaviours occurring as a result of the child's difficulty with the movement? If the movement is seen to be enjoyable and meaningful and a situation a child might encounter in everyday life, it is more likely to achieve success. Human movement has many dimensions. All children want to exploit the body's capacity for movement and they all delight in their accomplishments. A young child uses movement as a means of learning about themselves and the physical world. Children enjoy physical accomplishment, however trivial it might seem in adults' eyes; they enjoy movement for its own sake. They experiment, apply and develop it in many different ways.

A movement pattern is a definite arrangement of muscle actions required to achieve a desired outcome, e.g. walking, throwing a ball, jumping in the air. The spatial and rhythmic components remain relatively constant and can be practised, and they are essential

to achieving the desired outcome. A movement pattern may be likene
plate which then becomes a basis for a number of specific skills. This
critical if learning is to take place. To be versatile in movement, childr
possible range of experience, with opportunities for frequent applicati

How can this be achieved?

Assessment at the end of a lesson supports pupils' learning, motivates pupils, provides context for the next lesson and promotes a positive approach to learning. This type of formative assessment needs to help the teacher identify poor motor ability as this can have a serious effect on behaviour and motivation in all areas of the curriculum. If the child keeps experiencing failure, frustration will set in, which in turn will lead to 'switch off'.

Assessment at the end of a series of lessons helps in the monitoring of pupils' progress and achievement. It should refer to the consolidation of learning and is less about the ongoing process and more about the product of that area of learning as a permanent addition to the skills and abilities of the pupil. Assessment at the end of a year helps in the reviewing of pupils' strengths and identifies areas for development, focuses on activity and personal development, and forms the basis for a report to pupils and parents about the progress each pupil has made in all aspects of the year's work.

In the National Curriculum for Physical Education (DfEE, 2000) attainment targets are used in the assessment of pupils. They set out the 'knowledge, skills and understanding that pupils of different abilities and maturities are expected to have at particular ages'. They consist of eight level descriptors of increasing difficulty. Each level descriptor describes the types and range of performance that pupils working at that level should characteristically demonstrate and teachers need to judge which description best fits the pupil's performance. See, for example, levels 1 and 2 below:

Level 1
Pupils copy, repeat and explore simple skills and actions with basic control and coordination. They start to link these skills and actions in ways that suit the activities. They describe and comment on their own and others' actions. They talk about how to exercise safely, and how their bodies feel during an activity

Level 2
Pupils explore simple skills. They copy, remember, repeat and explore simple actions with control and coordination. They vary skills actions and ideas and link these in ways that suit the activities. They begin to show some understanding of simple tactics and basic compositional ideas. They talk about differences between their own and others' performance and suggest improvements. They understand how to exercise safely, and describe how their bodies feel during different activities.

order to use these level descriptors, teachers of children with movement difficulties including developmental coordination disorder will need to adopt flexible assessment strategies to be able to deliver them. An example of this could be linking the statements in with the Movement ABC. This would give a far more rounded picture of the level the child was working at. The levels include the children describing and commentating on their own work and that of others – this gives the child more 'ownership' of the task, and might identify the child who actually understands the movement but is not controlled at carrying out the task. In level 1, copying, repeating and exploring simple actions can include things like posture and using simple games to explore changes of speed and direction to improve control and consistency. These games can also include jumping, hopping and skipping, which will involve various degrees of balance and transfer of weight. These types of movement underpin much more complex tasks, so including them in a fun way and showing that the tasks have a purpose makes them far more likely to be successful. If throwing tasks are being practised, using targets of different sizes and different distances is far more enjoyable than throwing at a wall or simply just throwing and catching. Varying the tasks although concentrating on the same skill will stop the children becoming bored and also help the teacher in forming an overall picture of the level the children are working at and the individual needs each child will require. Getting the children to describe how their bodies feel during exercise is also helping them to understand what happens to their bodies. These actions fit into the visual, audio, kinaes-thetic model of learning. They are observing themselves and others, listening to feedback and giving feedback on their observations, and describing how their bodies feel during the tasks. This is getting them to focus on each individual action so they are able to understand how it affects the rest of their body.

How is it possible to assess all the different kinds of movement?

As stated above, getting the assessment right is of vital importance. There are many ways of assessing movement and using the level descriptors above with the Movement ABC in conjunction with the Special Educational Needs Code of Practice (DfES, 2001) is a good starting point. The more information that can be gathered the easier it becomes to set specific targets which can form the basis of an individual education plan (IEP). This plan identifies a pupil's immediate learning needs by assessing their progress against these targets. Again this is a continuous process to ensure progression and to indicate what future action might be taken.

It is better to have a small number of tasks to assess at any one time. Each group is chosen because the assessment evidence the teacher has gathered shows these are pre-sent problems. With small steps and progressions the child will build up a large collection of different skills and movement patterns. Breaking down the skills in this manner keeps the child constantly challenged and also helps them to understand the learning process. The children need to be encouraged to ask questions about their tasks, allowing them to make decisions and plan their actions. The children need to have space to be able to practise the skills before being thrown into group activities, which often makes them lose focus. It is sometimes a good idea to let the children decide how they wish to perform the tasks, allowing them some ownership of the activity.

The level descriptors are a way of helping to look at the whole child and how they respond to various situations, not just their motor abilities. It is looking at the process of how the child performs, not just the end result. This again helps in building up the picture of the child, seeing how it makes the child feel when they are successful and listening to their comments on how they performed. The objective is to gain as much detailed and specific evidence as possible concerning the child. Through the provision of clear structures the child is able to understand and help to take control of the learning situation.

Movement provides a two-way channel of learning, being both a way of finding out and a form of accomplishment. Indeed movement should not only be associated with or isolated within physical education, it happens in a multitude of everyday situations. In the process of moving, thought, feeling and perception combine to transfer impulse into appropriate action, again relating back to see, hear and feel.

Using appropriate assessments

For assessment to be accurate and worthwhile certain areas need to be addressed. Caroll (1994) and Bailey (2001) summed them up as follows:

Validity

The teacher assesses accurately what is supposed to be assessed. The skills, knowledge and understanding have to match the learning objectives of a lesson or unit. It also involves using a reliable strategy to measure what is to be assessed. Children with movement difficulties might have a problem with the planning of a movement sequence and not the execution of the skill therefore the child's problems are in the knowing, so the accuracy of the assessment is vital in identifying this area.

Reliability

This should ensure consistency of measurement under the same conditions. This is important if the process is to be seen as fair. The outcome should be the same, whichever teacher makes the assessment. This should include planning and decision-making skills.

Objectivity

This is related to reliability in so far as the assessment should not reflect personal or institutional prejudices. Avoiding assessing just the end result and not the process of the learning is an important focus here: a child who has a problem with the performance might be able to plan and make decisions well and therefore good focused observation skills are needed. It is also important not to let a child's behaviour get in the way of assessing the skills and movement patterns.

Practicality

Too many schemes of assessment are time-consuming and take much needed teaching time away. Therefore the teacher needs to find a practical blend between the demand for detail and the practicality of the lesson. Little and often is probably easier in the assessment of each child rather than large blocks of time once or twice a week. This also helps the child incorporate the skills into their daily routines. If the task is meaningful and fun the child is more likely to be successful.

According to Stillwell and Wilgoose (1997, p. 307) assessment in the adapted physical education programme for individual children serves the following purposes:

Screening   to determine which pupils are in need of help.

Placement   to assure that each pupil needing help is in the proper environment.

Diagnosis   to determine the present level of performance of each pupil to guide both the selection of activities and instruction.

Progress   to determine if the behavioural objectives have been met.

These criteria can be used in schools as part of the baseline assessment of all groups of children. If expected progress is not being made against the targets set, further action might include help from outside agencies to help the teachers in reassessing the problems.

The Movement ABC (Henderson and Sugden, 1992), as discussed in Chapter 3, is a battery of tests with planned interactions that make the tests more meaningful. The checklist is a screening instrument (for use by teachers) as well as a means for planning intervention. The motor part of the checklist is divided into four sections (12 items in each section) and represents the interaction between the child and the environment. Scores for each item are marked on an ordinal scale 0 to 3 and a total score is calculated with higher scores indicating impairment.

Factor analysis indicated that there were seven factors involved:

1 ball skills (by far the most important, accounting for 49.6 per cent of the variance);

2 static balance, manipulation of fine objects and keeping rhythm;

3 dynamic balance;

4 fine manipulation;

5 avoiding objects or persons;

6 knowledge of body scheme and directional awareness (including vehicle riding);

7 self care skills.

The implications of this seem to be that we should resist the use of a single category for children who have perceptual motor problems, but rather look for relatively specific training based on meaningful targets in real contexts which will be useful to children (either in terms of their educational skills or independence). This has been supported by a recent intervention study by Chambers and Sugden (2003), where the emphasis was on children performing functional tasks in settings that were as near as possible to everyday life.

However, more qualitative methods are needed to gain the full picture with a move away from assessment at the end of a unit of work to an understanding that assessment can inform and improve performance throughout the unit. Thus teachers need more than good assessment instruments; they also need help with methods to interpret and respond to the results in a formative way. The structure of tests therefore needs to reveal the methods used by those tested to provide teachers with the feedback to best help their pupils.

When applying formative assessments to provide positive results there needs to be a culture of success. This needs to be backed by a belief that everyone can achieve. Formative assessment 'provides information which can aid further progress, diagnose reasons for both good and poor performance, and target particular learning needs' (Capel, 2001, p. 289). For assessment to be formative the feedback information has to used, i.e. feedback has to be meaningful and realistic. If a child with poor motor development is left alone they will develop slowly and not be able to use skills required for daily life. If the child is presented with situations which help them learn in both an intentional and incidental manner then the child learns new skills forming a positive influence on their development. In school the so-called 'clumsy child' can stand out from the rest. Early experiences of failure can result in a child having little confidence in learning new skills.

An essential skill needed by teachers to formatively assess pupils is that of observation. Through observation teachers can adjust the tasks in order to match the needs of the individuals. However, Peach and Bamforth (2002, p. 52) highlighted that 'poor observational skills such as carelessness and lack of attention to detail and not applying selective attention may cause the task to be adjusted to the incorrect ability of the child.' Good observation is dependent on having clear criteria arising from learning objectives. Observing well is dependent on having a number of skills that require practice.

Conclusion

The importance of assessment has been clearly supported by many writers (Capel, 2004; Piotrowski, 2000; Sugden et al., 1993). Yet despite its importance, the quality and use of assessment data, particularly in physical education, was an area of concern according to the Ofsted (2002) annual report, with only one in ten schools being judged as 'good' in terms of PE assessment. The explanation behind this suggests that weaknesses are a consequence of poor or inefficient planning, which fails to clearly specify objectives against which pupils' work will be assessed. Furthermore, teachers are often preoccupied with what pupils have to do as opposed to what they are intended to learn (Ofsted, 2002).

Assessment should focus upon what pupils learn and how well they learn it. This information then becomes the basis for future planning and provides teachers with vital information on their own performance as a teacher.

Carroll (1994) implies that assessment always involves making a judgement. Assessment does not simply record what pupils have done in a lesson, but also makes some sort of qualitative statement as well. While there is a wide choice of different assessment procedures these need to be decided on the basis of the purpose for which the assessment is being undertaken. This may well mean employing different techniques for different assessment purposes.

The first role of assessment, then, is improving teaching and learning. Assessment can give feedback to children, which can help them progress and also allow the teacher to evaluate their effectiveness by assessing how well the learning objectives have been achieved. Learning objectives are specific statements that set out exactly what you want the children to learn. They form the intention or purpose of the lesson and are realised through the content selected and the learning experiences given to the pupils. This process helps the teacher to confirm whether there are any problems associated with a child's movement abilities. Secondly, it can indicate the nature and level of children's achievement or difficulties at specific points in their school life, for example a level from the physical education National Curriculum (2000) grade descriptors. Thirdly, it can be used for diagnostic purposes – this is especially important in detecting special needs in particular areas. It can also help to identify strengths and weaknesses which will inform planning and teaching. This is assessing the process and not just the end result.

It is apparent in this short chapter that learning and assessment go hand in hand – in other words if we teach children a basic movement pattern it is necessary for the teacher to assess the child's ability to perform the task. If the task is shown to be meaningful to the child and will enhance their everyday life then the assessment and feedback become very important. This is imperative to all teachers if learning is to progress and movement patterns and motor skills are to develop. Identifying specific problems early can really help a child improve their movement vocabulary. If this information is shared with parents and other professionals, for example the paediatric occupational therapist, a plan of action can be developed and an individual education plan written that is meaningful and enjoyable.

Developing Handwriting for Children with Coordination Difficulties

Sheila E. Henderson

Handwriting is a skill that takes time and effort to perfect, and some children with coordination difficulties can find this hard to master. This chapter outlines ways to help children understand and overcome their problems.

Movement is a fundamental component of human life. The ability to make precisely controlled movements is so much part of daily living that we are barely conscious of the countless motor acts we perform during our waking hours. Indeed, under normal circumstances, we only become aware of the intricacy of our movements when suddenly deprived of our skill, as in the attempt to coordinate the actions of hands and feet when learning to drive, or to sign a cheque, with icy cold fingers.

Although most children acquire the movement skills required of them at home and at school with ease, there is a small proportion for whom this area of learning will be an uphill struggle. Among this small group, some will arrive in school with their disability already labelled; others may be given a label at some point in their school career. Yet others may never receive one. Among those bearing a diagnostic label, we shall find children with Developmental Coordination Disorder (DCD), ADHD, dyslexia, Asperger syndrome and many others. Whatever the label, however, *handwriting* will be a skill which most dyspraxics will find extraordinarily difficult to master. Moreover, difficulty with handwriting will be something which not only affects academic attainment but may also affect self-esteem and emotional well-being.

The handwriting shown in Fig. 5.1 was produced by three boys over the age of eleven. None has severe learning difficulties, none has a severe physical disability and all are in mainstream schools. In fact:

- all three are very bright with verbal IQs above 120;

- all are fluent readers, with reading ages well above their chronological age;

- all have movement difficulties extending beyond their handwriting problems;

- all come from supportive home backgrounds.

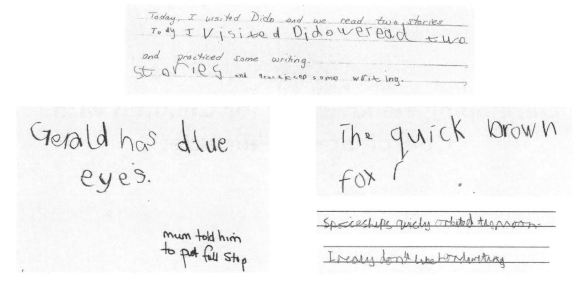

Figure 5.1   Handwriting produced by two children with movement difficulties.

In secondary school, these boys are likely to struggle. In addition to the fact that their writing is often very difficult to read, slowness of production causes many problems. All three children will find it difficult to get their homework down in time and to take notes in class. In free writing tasks, they may never be able to do themselves justice.

In trying to help children whose handwriting affects their progress in school, teachers have some difficult decisions to make. One of the most important is to decide at what point to consider substituting an alternative mode of communication, such as a laptop, rather than persevere with handwriting. In this chapter, there is space only to consider the option of trying harder with handwriting. Don't wait for the occupational therapist to come to school. For a great many children, the teacher's help will suffice.

The cognitive-motor approach: a strategy for understanding and remediating handwriting difficulties

Handwriting is a complex skill involving a wide range of cognitive, linguistic and perceptual-motor skills. It is the recording on paper of thoughts expressed in language, and writing systems vary according to the language used (see Fig. 5.2).

Children do not simply learn the conventions of their writing system automatically as if they were learning to run or hop. The required movements have to be taught in a well-structured way, from the beginning. Even with expert tuition, however, handwriting is a skill that takes time and effort to perfect and it is sometimes hard for teachers to decide when a child is falling too far behind his peers. However, experienced teachers can make such judgements and it is then necessary to consider what action should be taken.

Figure 5.2 Examples of one sentence written in six different languages, some with very different production rules.

Assessment and intervention always go hand in hand but never more so than in understanding and assisting children with handwriting difficulties. Assessment and intervention also form a partnership. Helping children to perceive and understand the nature of their own problems frequently suggests a first step towards their solution. To illustrate one possible strategy for making a plan of action, it is necessary to create an imaginary situation. Assume for a moment that you are a SENCo who has been asked to see a child for the first time. The child is 11 years old. He writes as shown in Fig 5.3.

61

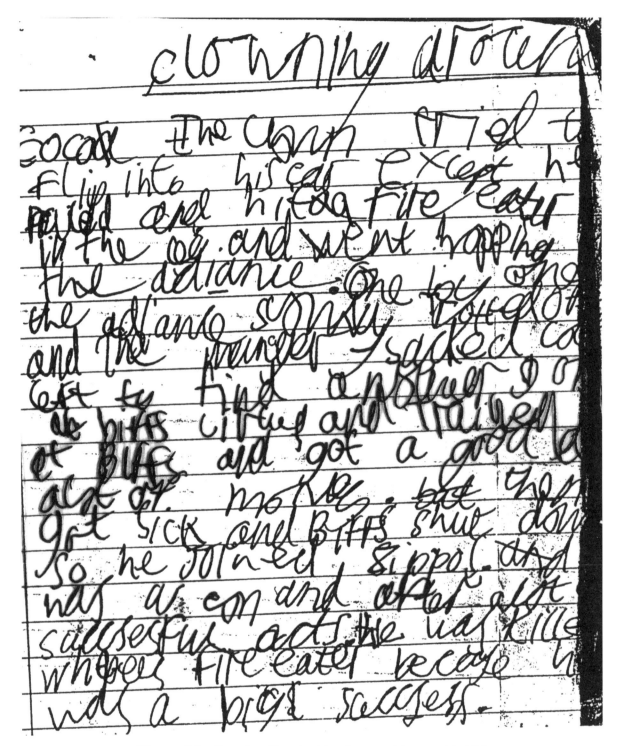

Figure 5.3 Sample of handwriting from an 11-year-old child.

The questions that need to be addressed can be grouped under three headings: (1) background information; (2) what can be learned from the finished product; and (3) what can be learned from watching the child.

62

Background information

This list could be long but most important for the SENCo are the following:

- a thorough knowledge of the school's policy on the teaching of handwriting – especially how handwriting is fitted into the National Literacy Strategy, the model used, provision for children with special needs and provision for children whose first language is not English;

- some idea of how the child's present teacher views handwriting, how much time is spent on formally teaching the skill, the importance attached to good presentation skills, etc.;

- some idea of the relevant previous experiences of the child, e.g. were other teachers concerned?

- an estimate of the child's level of skill in other aspects of literacy, e.g. in reading, spelling and composition (including SATS results);

- insight into other problems (e.g. in attention, concentration, motivation) that might affect progress.

What can be learned from the finished product?

Although it will eventually be crucial to spend time watching a child write, some preliminary information can be gained from studying a piece of writing beforehand (this can be done with the child alongside or in your own time). Think of the problems as falling into two overlapping categories: those arising from faults of *concept* and those arising from faults of *control*.

Faults of concept

The way we **form letters**, **and join them into words and sentences** in English is far from universal across languages. Children have to learn our own conventions from the beginning and have to be taught the particular movements required to form (and join) our letters. Often, this is taught by organizing letters into families according to shared features, e.g. *i*, *l*, *t*, *u*, *y*, *j* are all based on a simple down stroke. Some children pick up these conventions easily and can soon transform their 'cognitive' images into 'motor' ones. Others find it harder.

Letter formation

From looking carefully at a child's writing it is often possible to work out which letters they cannot form properly and/or which joins are a problem. This conclusion must then be confirmed by observation so that the errors the child makes can be described and corrected.

Spacing between words

Another aspect of our own writing system that differs from many others is in the representation of word boundaries using **spaces**. Some children learn this convention easily and soon insert an 'o' sized space between words without thinking. Children who leave no spaces at all may simply not understand the convention. Others may have odd ideas about how much to put on a line, etc. Ask the child! He may be able to tell you what was in his mind when he started well then squeezed everything together at the end of the line. As with letter formation, however, any hypothesis you have formed will have to be confirmed by direct observation.

Faults of control

Some children do not 'know' what to do. Others have the knowledge but cannot make their hands do what they would like them to do, fluently and accurately. Thus we may find children whose letter formation is actually accurate but who still produce very untidy illegible writing. From a finished piece of writing, we can make a list of this kind of fault (ask the child to help you). What should be included?

Alignment

The main body of a child's writing must 'sit on a line' (other writing systems 'hang down' from a line). Without getting into the debate about lined versus unlined paper, we may define the teacher's objective as always getting the child to understand the relationships between the main body of the letters and their ascenders and descenders. So, when analysing a child's written work, they must examine the main body of the writing, drawing in a straight line if necessary then marking the letters that deviate from this line. Having done this, it will next be necessary to look at the ascenders and descenders but this may best be done in the context of size.

Size

Here, we might start by looking at the main bodies of the letters again and asking whether they are too large, too small or too variable. For example, a single letter such as *a* might be chosen and the child asked to mark each one and decide whether they are all the same but too small, too large or too different from one occasion to another. Then look at the ascenders and descenders – do they show clearly above the main body of the writing, do they show clearly below or are they too inconsistent?

Slant/slope

There are a few children who produce writing that is very consistent but is illegible because it slopes too far back or too far forward. By far the most common problem, however, is inconsistent slope. In particular, many find it hard to make the ascenders and descenders consistent.

Tremor

Shakiness is something which is easy to observe in a child's writing but difficult to understand unless the child is known to have one of a number of medical conditions. Make a note of it and wait until you get to know the child better before planning any remedial action.

Pressure

Pressing too hard (or more rarely, insufficient pressure) on the paper is also a problem which shows up in the finished product but can only be fully understood from watching the child write. Make a note and wait.

Now that you have been able to look at the child's product in the absence of time constraints, it is time to observe the process of writing. This can be difficult as the child's posture might block your view or he may not like being watched, etc. However, these problems are soluble and having conducted the above analysis, you should have a few ideas about what exactly you want to see.

Watching the child write – the crucial stage

Before the child sits down to write, you must decide on the task to be performed. Since your primary focus (at least initially) must be on the handwriting itself rather than on other factors which might be affecting performance, such as a spelling problem, choose something to write that is conceptually easy for the child – perhaps starting with writing the alphabet and the numbers 1 to 10, then doing a simple copying task and/or writing a familiar poem that the child is able to recite without error. Place yourself in a position that allows you to observe the child as clearly as possible and be prepared to discuss the child's difficulties with him.

Faults of concept

Now is your opportunity to observe the child constructing each letter, by itself and linked with other letters, in context. You will know whether and how the child has been taught to join letters and should be able to record the kinds of difficulty he experiences with this. For example, it may be that the child can manage letters based on a down stroke but cannot manage those based on an oval or circle (o, c, a, etc.). Ask the child if he knows about letter families and which goes with which. Ask him if he knows about different kinds of joins (e.g. which letters join at the top). Demonstrate a letter, or pair of letters, you think he forms 'wrongly' and see if he can copy your correct demonstration, and so on.

Similarly, use your detective skills to get to the bottom of the child's understanding of spacing between (and within) words. Does he fail to manage the spacing of his writing properly because he does not understand the convention or because of a problem with movement control?

All teachers should be skilled at task analysis. Carry on with this process until you are clear whether the child needs to 'return to basics' and learn once again how to form letters or whether the main problem is one of control of the process of execution.

Faults of control

Although I have thus far emphasised the cognitive aspects of handwriting, it is also crucial to remember that writing is a movement skill, like playing the piano, typing or playing tennis. This means we have to think of the design of the movements and how they are controlled.

Posture, pen grip and paper position

Children adopt all sorts of odd postures when writing. They may lie on the floor, sit on a foot, lie on an arm, etc. They also hold the writing implement in very different ways. Some will write well and some will write not so well. What is clear is that there is no one-to-one relationship between posture, pen grip and legibility of writing. However, when a child is having difficulty we must attempt to determine what aspects of their posture and pen grip might be making life more difficult for them. In particular, posture and pen grip affect the fluency and speed with which a child can write.

One way of observing a child's overall posture is to start with the head and eyes. Ask yourself whether the child's head (and therefore the eyes) are too close or at an odd angle to the paper. Then consider the arms and hand. Ask yourself whether the arms are positioned correctly on the desk and how these relate to the position of the head. Make a note of the kind of grip the child is using and try to determine whether this allows the child to move the fingers easily on the pen and the hand fluently across the page. Now, look at the child's sitting posture. Ask yourself whether he looks comfortable and stable, with his feet firmly on the floor. Be sure, at this point, to assess the school furniture. Ask yourself whether the chair is too low or too high, whether the desk is too low or too high, whether its slope is adequate. (Fig. 5.4) Finally, ask the child whether he feels comfortable writing, whether he gets headaches or his hand hurts when he writes a lot. Once you have gathered this information proceed to consider the following.

Figure 5.4 Good posture cannot be achieved without appropriately sized furniture – would you like to sit like this for much of the day?

Pressure and fluency

Many children with handwriting difficulties press too hard upon the paper and/or find it difficult to execute fluent movements. Sometimes these two problems are linked, sometimes not. For the child who presses too hard, you must first work out where the excessive pressure comes from. Is it the consequence of an awkward and static grip, does the pressure travel through the whole arm, or is because the child himself is generally tense (emotionally and, therefore, physically too). In either case, the child will find it hard to move fluently. At this point you might want to experiment with an easily flowing felt tip pen or a piece of chalk on a large piece of paper – see if the child can shed his tightness and make huge circles or ovals, draw you a picture, etc.

There are other children whose movements are spiky and awkward but who do not press too hard on the paper. Their handwriting may be irregular in all sorts of ways, exhibiting variable size, slope or alignment, even when they can form the letters adequately. This problem can sometimes be quite easily solved by allowing the child to experiment with different sizes of writing. Start large (perhaps with a single guideline for alignment) and work towards smaller writing. Only work on one dimension at a time and, whenever you see any tension creeping in, back off and emphasize fluency again.

Speed

Assessing the speed of a child's handwriting is not a simple problem and merits an essay in itself. It is vital for a school to have procedures in place for ensuring that children who need to have special arrangements made for exams are provided for. This includes those who are unable to attain adequate writing speed.

At a bare minimum, you should know how many letters per minute a child can produce when writing the alphabet (an over-learned task) and how many words per minute are produced in a conceptually undemanding free writing task (write about your favourite person for 20 minutes). Norms are available for these tasks.

Conclusion

There are many excellent texts around which deal with assessment and intervention for children with handwriting difficulties. In this chapter, what I have tried to do is emphasize the *cognitive* aspects of the task as well the *motor* demands. Knowing 'what to do' is a prerequisite for working out 'how to do it' but fluent execution comes to the child neither immediately nor automatically. For an intervention programme to be successful, teachers must view these two kinds of problems as interacting with each other over time and they must develop problem-solving strategies that accommodate difficulties of both sorts.

The National Handwriting Association

The National Handwriting Association (Chairman Sheila Henderson) has a comprehensive range of resources for helping schools to deliver this vital aspect of the curriculum. Below are some examples that schools may wish to consider.

Publications

The National Handwriting Association produces a series of booklets and other materials designed to foster good handwriting practice and help with handwriting difficulties. These include

- **Which Handwriting Scheme?** The National Handwriting Association has produced this publication to help readers to find the best scheme for their needs. It reviews 15 currently available handwriting schemes published in the UK. Each scheme is summarized, its aims are stated and some pages are reproduced so that teachers can see how much detail is given on the worksheet. Important stages in teaching, such as joining, are addressed, and the style of writing used. ISBN 1-872832-18-0.

- **Handwriting – Are You Concerned?** Primarily written for parents, this booklet covers the basics of teaching handwriting together with suggestions for what to do when there is cause for concern. Now in its second edition, it has proven a useful resource for all professionals. ISBN 1-872832-94-6.

- **Tools of the Trade.** The worker is only as good as his tools! This booklet provides a comprehensive guide to the principles on which the selection of pens, pencils, paper and other writing equipment should be based. ISBN 1-872832-99-7.

- ***Handwriting in the Secondary School.*** This booklet is written primarily for teachers who want to help secondary pupils to develop better handwriting (Key Stages 3 and 4) and includes sections on identifying and supporting pupils in the secondary school. It also includes a section on keyboarding skills as well as information regarding special examination arrangements ISBN 1-872832-89-X.

- ***Hands Up for Handwriting!*** Flexible fingers and relaxed hands help to made handwriting fluent and flowing. This photocopiable sheet provides, in a simple-to-follow format, a series of exercises to prepare the hands for handwriting. They are fun to do and easily performed while sitting at a desk.

- ***Developing a Handwriting School Policy.*** This book provides schools with an overview of how to incorporate handwriting into the framework of the National Curriculum. It raises the issue of identification and intervention approaches for children who have difficulties recording work. It also gives step-by-step guidance for schools when developing their handwriting school policy ISBN 1-872832-21-0.

Handwriting Today

Handwriting Today is a journal produced by the National Handwriting Association annually and is mailed free to members. The journal contains a variety of good articles including pieces on practice and research that is taking place across the country. Examples include a research project carried out into the handwriting practice in a number of schools in the Brighton and Hove area. In another article, a paediatric therapist explains the merits of 'The Tool Box' which includes a variety of the most commonly used equipment for helping children with poor fine motor skills. This was introduced to schools in the Isle of Man to help children with special educational needs.

The journal also includes a review section of some of the latest handwriting/keyboard equipment as well as publications in this field.

Courses

The National Handwriting Association has launched a course designed to suit as many professionals as possible interested in the teaching of handwriting. The course is offered as an optional module on the Advanced Diploma in Education or as a free-standing accredited module (30 credits) for those registered on other courses. The course runs over five days. Sessions include:

- the basics of handwriting;

- assessment of children's handwriting;

- alternative methods for recording children's handwriting.

Short courses

The National Handwriting Association also holds a series of short courses in London, Cardiff and other venues across the country.

Training

If you are involved in Inset coordination for an LEA or school and would be interested in specific training workshops in the area of handwriting, contact the Inset Chair Person (details can be found on the website below).

Information

For further information about any of these resources contact:

www.nha-handwriting.org.uk

A section of this chapter appeared in *Special Magazine*, the official magazine of NASEN. Copyright Solutions Publishing Ltd. All rights reserved.

Developing a Gross Motor Programme for Children with Coordination Difficulties

Christine Macintyre

Running and jumping, swinging and climbing, catching and kicking a ball – these are just some of the things children love to be able to do. All the better if these skills develop at the same time as their friends because then they can join in their games, practising and learning and becoming more skilled as they do.

This leads to a gain in confidence and children's self-esteem is boosted to the extent that they can become leaders, suggesting new games or ways to solve problems. In turn accumulating these experiences helps develop their imagination and their potential to reflect and learn. Success built upon these happenings means that children can become eager players, alert and ready to meet new challenges across all the different aspects of learning. They can make new friends by sharing activities (social learning); they can learn to appreciate the 'rules' of a game (intellectual learning); they can improve and extend their movement abilities and skills (motor learning) and through all of that become more confident and self-assured (emotional learning).

But of course not all children can move easily in different environments. Some stumble and fall and permanently have skinned knees and bruised egos. These are the children who can't sit still, who barge into others and who find it difficult to arrive anywhere in time! Their self-esteem flounders as they find they are unable to do what the other children do and this is exacerbated by the fact that movement is public, open to the scrutiny of their not always altruistic friends. Very often they become so tired from trying to change, yet their bodies cannot conform. This is because they lack the balance, the coordination and the control (the capacity to use strength and timing appropriately) to comply. It is a sad fact that 6–10 per cent of our children fall into this latter category and tragic that the numbers of children with movement learning difficulties are increasing. Keen (2001) claims that there is an 80 per cent increase in the number of children with learning difficulties and poor movement is one co-occurring feature of them all (Macintyre and Deponio, 2003). It is important that steps to help these children are taken now before all aspects of their learning are impaired, especially if, as Cowden and Eusson (1991) claim, 'intervention to help movement may take longer than other difficulties'.

What can schools do to support children who cannot move effectively and efficiently in different environments?

The first important move is to observe the children carefully to find the kinds of skills they lack. This is not easy as movement is quickly over and many eyes have not been trained to 'see' what is amiss. Luckily most schools now have a video camera that can record the children's movements. The video allows repeated viewing; staff can discuss the film together so that several pairs of eyes can compare and contrast their observations and the film can also be used to show progress over time. This is tangible evidence that provides the observers with confidence in the assessments they have made and invaluable material if referral to an outside expert becomes justified.

What do children need to know before they can be competent or efficient movers?

A basic movement skill depends on a child knowing:

> *What to move, where to move, when to move, how to use feedback from one try to help the next and above all how to stay safe.*

And indeed these are the factors that provide a complete analysis of movement. *Knowing what to move*, i.e. what body part to coordinate, involves the children in planning, organizing and sequencing, competences that depend on a good sense of where the different parts of the body are in relation to each other. So if children are having difficulties it might well be that underlying competence which is preventing them becoming skilled. Lots of body awareness games (see MacIntyre, 2003) can complement the old favourites, e.g. 'Heads, shoulders, knees and toes' (add bottoms, back and nose to help children know where their backs are!) and games such as 'Simon Says'.

But how does the observer know if it is planning and organizing that is 'faulty'? That process is hidden unless the children are asked to share their thoughts. Asking them 'Tell me what you are going to do first then next' lets the practitioner see if the planning matches the outcome and also ensures that any intervention is appropriate, not based on helping the wrong dimensions. Practitioners must listen as well as watch if there is any suspicion that a planning and organizing deficiency exists.

Knowing when to move is a timing decision that many children find difficult. Even adults can find it difficult to get onto or off an escalator without concentrating hard, especially if a case is held in one hand. Many young children attempting to catch a ball will clutch thin air after it has flown past. They have moved their arms too late. This is a timing decision.

Timing affects the rhythm of a movement phrase. In efficient movement the rhythm should be smooth and fluent. How can this rhythmic sense be developed? One way is to ask children to listen to the sound of their feet on the floor. In running to jump over a rope as just one example, the rhythm will tell if the approach run has been too rapid and the child is likely to run through the rope because there has been too much speed (momentum) to allow control or if the run-up has not been quick enough there may not be enough power to take the body into the flight of the jump. Even considering the turning of the jump in flight, i.e. noting the time between take-off and landing can help, because this tells if the take-off has been too near, too far away or just right.

Knowing how to move is based on the 'what and the when', i.e. on sound body awareness and timing skills. It also involves awareness of dominance, i.e. recognizing and using the 'best' hand or foot for the task to be done. Knowing how also concerns the poise of the body in stillness and in movement – attributes that derive from a sense of balance (the vestibular sense).

Knowing where to move concerns the spatial aspects of movement. Spatial decision-making is part of every action that takes the body away from the spot. If children make faulty judgements about whether they can pass between two desks then they will be bumped and bruised, if they misjudge the riser of a step they will topple down and if they see the edge of the kerb as further away than it really is then falls into the road could be the tragic result.

All of these kinds of actions should be practised in simple then in increasingly complex situations.

Setting out apparatus

Practitioners have different important responsibilities in setting out apparatus. These are:

- providing crash mats under any apparatus where there is the slightest possibility of a fall;

- judging the approach distance needed between different pieces of apparatus and ensuring that approach runs and landings don't cross;

- ensuring that the correct number of children are allowed on the climbing frame at once;

- providing apparatus arrangements that hold different levels of challenge.

Apparatus arrangements should be set out so that observers can see the children crawling, walking, running, jumping, swinging and climbing, for these are the basic movement patterns which underlie all composite gross movement patterns. Barrels can show if the children can crawl through and pull out. These are incredibly important skills. If the children can crawl it shows they have the cross-lateral coordination and sequencing (which limb moves first?) necessary to travel along the ground. Pulling out is a good test of arm strength and both of these are essential components of being able to write – a skill that requires the children to cross the midline of their bodies. This can be impossible for some children, necessitating much practice of figure of eight type movements.

The movement abilities that have been identified are:

- body and spatial awareness;

- balance;

- coordination;

- rhythm;

- control.

No matter how safe the apparatus is and no matter the different levels of challenge that are provided, some children will be wary of joining in. How can they be encouraged? Asking the children to observe and be 'teachers' can help their understanding of the planning and organizing side of movement thus building up their knowledge ready for when they have the confidence to take part. Interactions like, 'Watch Ben, where should he place his hands so that he can give a long pull along the bench?' or 'What apparatus should we choose for running then jumping then rolling?' or asking children to suggest ideas, e.g. 'Tell me how you think we might build up a fireworks dance' can give 'poor movers' a real sense of achievement and hopefully encourage them to participate in the practical side of things.

Children who can suggest good ideas can even be encouraged to help teachers plan the movement programme for the term, because they can suggest classroom links, e.g. dramatic activities based on classroom themes such as 'the sea' (waves, rocks, seaweed, fish, dolphins, mermaids or pirates) or 'Machines' (cog wheels, piston rods, levers, oil cans). The children can select music or percussion to accompany the movement and have turns of being in charge of and playing the tape recording or the tambourine. This develops listening skills, observation skills and rhythmical appreciation. There are many subtle ways to involve children who are reluctant to move.

All children, skilled movers or not, need to be helped to recognize how they are progressing. They must be enabled to receive genuine praise for their efforts so that their self-esteem can be kept afloat. Having different tasks can widen the possibility of each child being told 'Well done, you have made real progress in your movement today'.

A frustrating difficulty can arise for everyone concerned if some children can't remember what they learned yesterday or if they can't transfer their movement learning from one situation to another. If they are to have any chance of doing that – and arguably this is the basis of real learning in the movement domain – then they must understand how movements can be adapted to different situations. Teachers need to spell out the essence of transfer, e.g. 'We are learning the best way to kick a ball in the gym so that when we go outside, we'll be able to score a goal. Remember that it is the same action, just the place that is different' or 'We are practising running then slowing down to stop at the chalk line. Remember how to do that when you have to stop at the kerb before you cross the road'. These interactions, which spell out how to transfer learning, need to be carefully prepared, and it is very important that this happens, as some children will not make the link and see each movement as a first time try, requiring a new and baffling set of skills. No wonder they get frustrated and tired!

Building a movement programme

General teaching points

Many schools have been encouraged by seeing a marked improvement in their children's movement and in their self-confidence (which transfers to confidence in classroom activities) after they have taken part in a daily movement programme. Whenever possible schools have arranged these programmes at the start of the day when the children are fresh. They last 20 minutes or so – just the length of time classroom administration takes. This means new learning is not missed. Some children volunteer to come in to school a few minutes early and this helps too.

Selecting the children for the movement programme

Going on the programme should be presented as a treat – children are chosen, not picked out! There are many children who can benefit from learning to move with poise and control. Those who can't be still can benefit even though they are skilled enough to climb trees. They learn how to control the pace of the action.

Children who can't pay attention can also develop through being in a small group and having more one-to-one attention than is possible in a classroom. This means that the movement group is not seen as 'something remedial' raising parents' and children's fears that something is wrong! But of course that ethos can only be put over by the staff.

Some general hints to help you start

- At the start of a new programme, begin with just a few children, perhaps those who need most support. This gives them extra practice and familiarizes them with the routine of the programme. Tell them they have been chosen to help you set up a programme and so 'we need to find good things to do'. Having a small number of children also gives the teacher more opportunities to carry out accurate observations.

- If the children are going into an unfamiliar space, limit the area with benches. A large area can be frightening for some children and causes others to 'go wild'. Letting off steam frightens the timid ones and doesn't help any child's movement to be improved at all.

- Once other children join in, the first group can be helpers, explaining what the others have to do. For children lacking confidence, this gives their self-esteem a real boost while at the same time recapping the purpose of the movements for them and so helping their movement memories!

■ Give the children selected for the programme small responsibilities/duties so that they feel genuinely involved. One child might get the tape recorder ready while another could 'collect one beanbag for each person from the cupboard'. Such tasks involve them in one-to-one correspondence and so help their mathematical problem-solving. This is more challenging and rewarding than asking the children to 'bring out four beanbags'. Teachers need to think out their ways of interacting as well as choosing the content of a programme.

■ Avoid having children choose teams because the same children will always be chosen last. Instead, have coloured bands and distribute them as children enter the hall. A little preplanning can ensure that the talent within each group is distributed fairly. Using bands can help organization even if teams are not necessary, e.g. 'The blue group sit on the benches for a moment to give the greens more space'.

■ Avoid competitions unless it is the 'beat your own score' kind. Competition leads to rushing, which defeats the purpose of careful planning.

■ Be positive. Thank the children for their efforts. Explain why they have done well, e.g. 'You've given me some really good ideas today', or 'Everyone worked very hard to control the ball/clap the rhythm/remember the words of the jingle. Well done'. This is much more helpful than a vague 'well done'. It is important that the children finish the activity session feeling they have made progress.

■ At the end of the session help them to reflect and remember, e.g. 'Everyone put your thinking cap on [physically pretend to do this] and don't let any of these good ideas escape till tomorrow'. Perhaps children with poor short-term memories can be asked to 'remember the best thing you did today and see if you can do it just as well tomorrow'. Back in the classroom, they could be encouraged to draw out the floor pattern which they followed as they moved or pictures of the apparatus or pictures of themselves throwing and catching. These drawings can be build into a movement book with descriptive words written alongside.

■ Always finish with a recap, e.g. 'Let's remember what we did today. There was … and … Haven't we done well?' Allowing the children to volunteer suggestions is much better that asking, 'Jon, what do you remember?' This is because Jon may have to admit publicity that he doesn't remember, or doesn't want to spell out anything at all.

Note, if benches and/or other heavy pieces of equipment are to be used, organise children from the older classes to come and help. Often children with poor muscle tone can be hurt or inadvertently cause accidents. It is good to remember that some 'disabilities' are not immediately apparent so teachers may think children look stronger than they are. In any movement programme, safety is *the* critical consideration. It goes without saying that benches have to be checked for wobbles and even worse, splinters, and that all apparatus is secure.

DEVELOPING A GROSS MOTOR PROGRAMME FOR CHILDREN WITH COORDINATION DIFFICULTIES

Programme ideas

Suggestions for a programme based on the basic movement patterns of crawling, walking, running, jumping, catching, kicking and aiming follow. These patterns should be done well on the floor before equipment is introduced.

A complementary/interchangeable programme can be based on dance/drama type movements which do not need equipment. The stories and jingles can act as the stimulus.

Some critical teaching points for any activity

- 'Stand for a moment and feel your balance before you begin.'

- 'Tell me what you are going to do … where you are going and which moves will need most care.'

- 'Can you picture the fast parts and the slow parts?'

- 'Where have you to take especial care?' (For example, bending the knees to land safely and being strong enough to spring up again.)

Standing, walking and marching

Many simple walking practices are fun and can be made more interesting with dramatic ideas, e.g. chocolate soldiers who march vigorously till they are too warm and melt (drooping and sinking to the floor).

Alternatively, accompanying movements with percussion or music can help the movement to be flowing and suggest changes in rhythm, speed and strength. Lines can be drawn or ropes laid out on the floor to ensure that children can turn corners and then change directions quickly.

Standing position
Standing still

The children should be able to stand still without rocking. Feet should be reasonably close with toes pointing forward. The back of the head should be up, the shoulders low and the trunk and legs extended.

Movements from standing

- Standing still, swinging arms back and forward together rhythmically, bending and straightening knees. As arms lift, link with breathing in. After some swings, hold arms high and still. Ask, 'Can you feel your fingertips (without looking)?'

  Progression: As you swing your arms up and hold them high, look up to see your fingertips (note any loss of balance). Swoop your arms down again. Make them heavy.

You have to hold on with your toes to keep balanced. Add walking forward on the lift and being still as the arms drop and build this into a sequence.

- Standing feet apart, well balanced. 'Can you feel a line drawn right down through your nose down your chest and your tummy, right to the floor?' Gradually shift entire weight onto one foot, regain symmetrical stance then shift weight over to the other side. Try to build up a sideways rhythmical shift without twisting the body.

    Progression: In twos (one supporting), take turns to balance on a wobble board.

- Stand facing a bench (broad side up). Push up high onto bench – right foot leading, step down, change feet, step up again left foot leading and down to two feet together. Push the top of the head high, keep shoulders down and try to look ahead. Count out the time the balance can be held without wobbling.

NB. Try to build up a rhythmical sequence in even the simplest activity because awareness of the intrinsic rhythm helps the movement to flow. This saves energy and makes the movement more efficient.

Standing games (to encourage the development of body awareness)

In twos, one lifts a hoop over the head of the second child and lowers it to the ground. The idea is not to touch the standing child. Vary the speed. Do it very slowly and very quickly. When the hoop reaches the ground it can be lifted up again, again without touching the child who is still. Then the children change over. To add to the fun and the difficulty, the child within the hoop can hold a fat toy or move a football, i.e. anything to add to the bulk! Another fun progression is for the standing child to change his position so that constant adjustments have to be made. He is not allowed however, to move his feet.

Crawling

Crawling should be part of every session as it promotes balance and spatial orientation as well as cross laterality. Examples are:

- crawling through a hoop to throw a beanbag into a bin (This involves lifting one hand – note the shift in balance);

- crawling *under* a rope (judging distance and space) and over a rolled up mat.

Kicking horse/bunny jumps

From the crawling position the children lean forward over their hand and after extending one leg, attempt to kick it into the air. The head should look forwards to help the balance.

If the children look back through their arms they will topple over. Arms, hands and fingers need to stay strong. Just have a few turns – this is tiring but the children love to try.

Teachers – note which leg is chosen and see if dominance is developing. Compare that to the development of hand dominance.

Rolling – sideways rolls from crawling

This is a safety practice that should first happen on mats. From the crawling or table position the children should tuck one arm through the other, follow it with their head and roll over onto their shoulder and back, sustaining enough momentum to roll right round to kneeling. The children should understand that they are taking their weight on the rounded padded bits and that elbows, the points of shoulders and knees need to be protected. They also need to realise that this skill, i.e. learning to meet the ground safely, will protect them should they fall. They must not fall on outstretched arms else jarring or even clavicle breakage may occur.

NB: Avoid forward rolls if the children have Down's syndrome as vertibrae in the neck might dislocate.

Walking

Walking in straight lines, forwards and backwards, then along curves and then with abrupt changes of direction. Check the smooth transfer of weight from heel to toe. Check that each leg shows equal strength. The children should be confident, not having to look down if there are no obstacles in their path.

Walking through the space made by two facing benches. The activity begins with the benches far apart and gradually moving together. The aim is for the children to be aware of objects at their side and to judge the width of their body/movement pattern in relation to the available space. (This develops spatial awareness and laterality or sidedness.)

Dramatic ideas to show a change of quality in walking

1 Build small-group (dramatic) activities based on walking. In these the quality of the walk should change, e.g.

   – On a cold frosty morning walk briskly to school.

   – Blow out to make 'frosty breath'. Blow on cupped hands. Shake tingling fingers (these actions can challenge balance).

   – Swoop arms around to keep warm (hand and back awareness).

   – See a friend and wave. Run over to join hands and jump up and down together to keep warm.

2   It is very hot in the rain forest. You are trying to spot exotic butterflies and humming birds.

- Prowl quietly through the undergrowth (slow careful walking at a low level).

- Use big sweeping actions to clear a path (balance challenge).

- Curl up quietly and listen to the humming sounds (change of level).

- Notice a snake slithering through the undergrowth (raise head, straighten arms).

- Jump up and rush away, leap up into your tree house (change of speed, balance challenge in jumping and crouching).

This can be built up into a dramatic dance (see below) if different children take different parts, e.g. humming birds, butterflies, snakes, leopards, macaws, etc. The children can describe a series of events and the teacher can add descriptive words linking a class theme and literacy development.

Building a dramatic dance

Action words	Teaching points
Prowl through the forest	Keep low, place each foot carefully, heel then toe (rocking action). Be very quiet.
Curl up small Listen hard – be very still Try not to move at all	Curl down onto the ground – gently, tuck in elbows and shoulders. Round your back and hide your face.
Stretch out as you rise right up	Gradual unfurling and stretching (balance challenge).
Jump up – very tall	Explosive jump as contrast.
Look out for hazards in your path, be careful not to fall.	This phrase gives the children a moment to find a well balanced position.
Rush home very quickly now	Change of pace – feet flit over the floor.
Never delay	As above.
Watch out for others in your path	Make sure you run into the spaces.
Show them the way!	Beckon/wave to the others and run home together.

Marching and marking time

Marching can be interspersed with **marking time** on the spot to give children time to regain their balance, to internalize the rhythm and to get ready to begin again. The teacher or a child can call out instructions such as:

'RIGHT TURN', 'HALT!', 'SALUTE!', 'FORWARD MARCH!', 'MARK TIME, HALT'.

The child calling out has to judge when it would be appropriate to change the command, e.g. when the spacing was poor or when a child fell over. This kind of game appeals to both boys and girls because doing things 'in time' and 'in line' has a novelty value for them. Marching often has more appeal to children than walking because of the strength and the exaggerated poise. It is very good for making them aware of where their body parts are and where they themselves are in relation to others in the room.

The children can march behind one another or alongside, keeping level or equally spaced out – whatever is appropriate. Marching side by side helps develop awareness/sidedness/laterality.

Lead in activity

Divide the class into two groups. The groups standing out can clap the rhythm with the teacher who should call out the instructions.

They can then change over. This is easier than having too many children on the floor at once in the early stages. Some children can be upset by too much bustle and some find changes of direction difficult.

Balance activities

- Walking along a bench without looking down, jumping off to land two feet together with 'bendy knees' (to absorb the weight and teach good landing technique).

- As above but stepping over spaced out bean-bags (toes should keep facing forward).

- Add a task at the end, e.g. collect a hockey stick/hoop from a box and carry it back along the bench. Pass it to another child who carries it back to the box. The hoop or stick can be carried in different ways, e.g. held out to the side, even overhead, thus developing balance challenges.

- Carrying out a series of bunny jumps over the bench from side to side, beginning at one end, and keeping the movement flowing till reaching the other end.

- Lie on front of bench. Stretch well ahead and pull body along. Try not to allow legs to go to the side.

- Make a sequence, e.g.

  - bunny jump along and balance walk back;

  - swivel on hips along and run back;

  - balance walk along with hoop held above the head; walk back slowly stepping in and out of hoop as you go.

Manipulative/ball skills

These include rolling and retrieving, throwing and catching, kicking and aiming.

NB. Some children can find a patterned background, glaring light or other children moving distracting as they try to track a ball and move to catch it. In the learning stages ensure that they are facing a blank wall so that they have every chance of seeing the approaching ball as early as possible.

Many children with motor learning difficulties do not have the hand-eye or foot-eye coordination or the balance to be able to be proficient in ball skills and yet most children yearn to be able to do them. Analyzing the sequence shows how complex these are and shows why children should practise basic actions before adding environmental hazards, e.g. learning to kick a stationary ball into a goalmouth before attempting to kick a moving one past a goalkeeper!

Releasing a ball at the right time is an essential component (a timing skill), as is being able to move to catch the ball (a tracking skill). The steps and stages outlined below provide one way to proceed.

Tunnels

In twos facing one another, sitting legs outstretched and apart. Roll the ball into the gap made by the other person's legs. This helps directionality and tracking skills and it's fun when the speed is varied. The good thing is that no time is lost chasing the ball to bring it back. It is firmly held in the tunnel. The distance between the children can be adjusted according to skill.

Then two join up

In groups, sit in a circle in the same position. The child with the ball chooses where to roll it and the receiver rolls the ball on into the next tunnel. Once the idea is understood, using two balls can give lots of laughs and surprises. All the children have to keep alert in case they are the one to receive the ball!

In these sitting activities, balance difficulties are removed. Releasing the ball and tracking its path are good practices for reading, and the uncertainly caused by not knowing where the ball is going to go keeps attention focused in the more difficult second activity.

- From standing, each child with a ball rolls it ahead and retrieves it before it reaches a line on the floor.
- Each child rolls a ball against the broad face of an upturned bench and retrieves it on the rebound. This helps judging speed, i.e. estimating the speed of the rebound in line with their ability to catch.

All these practices help timing the release of the ball and making a judgement about how much speed and strength to use. The children see the effect of their actions. They are also required to make a basket and to move in line with the oncoming ball to catch it. The individual children are still in total control, not depending on a partner to roll sympathetically.

Throw and catch sympathetically to a partner

The children will need to be helped with the distance between the partners and be shown the stance (opposing foot forward) that allows the long, smooth arm movement of the underarm throw. Although this sounds easy, children with poor three-dimensional vision will turn away rather than catch because seeing the approaching ball late may mean that they do not have time to make adjustments. If this happens allow them to use a foam ball.

The children can set up mini competitions where they try to beat their own record, e.g. aiming for five throws and catches without dropping the ball.

NB. Some children will find *bouncing* the ball to one another easier – they have more time to adjust their position to make the catch.

Try putting rice in a balloon and use that as a starter for children who find throwing and catching difficult. A brightly coloured balloon helps tracking too!

Skittle alley

Rolling the ball to knock down skittles helps aiming – this can be called ten-pin bowling if 'alleys' are constructed. Younger children can make and decorate their skittles from tubes filled with sand. These will topple more easily than the gym ones which are harder to knock over.

Use a variety of balls as skill improves. Foam balls travel more slowly and are easily retrieved, but they don't have much 'go'. Volleyballs are best because they are the 'real thing' but are light enough not to hurt. This activity is good for organization and planning – and also for waiting to take turns and letting one or two others finish their turn before the skittles can be set up again.

Mini practices that can suffice when children are waiting turns on the 'real' skittle alley can be simply constructed, e.g. rolling a tennis ball into an upturned bucket. This helps aiming skills, tracking and also with the stance which is the same for rolling and throwing.

Kicking

Most children love to kick a ball and will happily practise. What the inexpert kicker does, however, is to run at the ball and use the point of the foot to send it off in any direction at any speed. To gain control, the children need to begin by standing by the ball and push it just a short distance into a net (to keep the game real), using the front of the inside of their preferred foot. This helps the direction of the kick to be more accurate and the ball goes into the net. Success! This also helps the children to judge the strength that is needed. Pushing the ball into an empty net (a closed skill) needs to be practised before a goalie is added because then two things, i.e. the ball and the position of the opponent, have to be considered as well. Finally the children can run to kick a stationary ball before getting to grips with a moving ball (an open skill). The terrain, e.g. whether it is rough or smooth, sloping or level, can affect the success and so this has to be part of the learning curve too.

Dribbling the ball round skittles is another form of kicking, and control and judging speed and distance are equally important. The distance between skittles will determine the number of changes of direction and the angle of change which is required, so the arrangement can be adjusted to suit the children's skill. Teachers should remember that in 'races', popular as they are, the skill is likely to disappear as the children become involved with the hustle and bustle of getting to the end and winning!

Batting

A good fun introduction can come about if the children use cardboard tubes (the insides of kitchen rolls) to bat a balloon back and forward. Control is difficult but there's lots of fun. The slower pace helps children see the approaching balloon and position themselves ready to make the hit.

Wooden bats and shuttlecocks give a very satisfactory 'thwack'. The rhythm can be heard and helps continuity.

Table tennis is excellent because it does not involve contact and the pace of the ball – which doesn't hurt – can be controlled by the players. *Aim – to get a rally of five hits* rather than to outwit a partner!

And so there are many ways to practise basic movement skills which underlie all the activities of daily living and learning. Helping children to achieve efficient movement will stand them in good stead. As they learn they need encouragement, praise and, above all, they should have fun.

Further activities for motor programmes

Suggestions for further activities for gross motor programmes may be found in the following publications:

Macintyre, C. (2001) *The Art of Action Research in the Classroom*. London: David Fulton.

Macintyre, C. (2000) *Dyspraxia 5–11*. London: David Fulton.

Macintyre, C. (2000) *Dyspraxia in the Early Years*. London: David Fulton.

Macintyre, C. (2002) *Early Intervention in Movement*. London: David Fulton.

Macintyre, C. (2002) *Enhancing Learning through Play*. London: David Fulton.

Macintyre, C. (2002) *Play for Children with Special Needs*. London: David Fulton.

Macintyre, C. (2003) *Jingle Time: Rhymes and Activities for Early Years' Learning*. London: David Fulton.

Macintyre, C. (2005) *Listen to the Children to Identify Their Special Needs*. London. Routledge.

Macintyre, C. and Deponio, P. (2003) *Assessing and Supporting Children with Specific Learning Difficulties. Looking Beyond the Label to Assess the Whole Child*. London: Routledge.

Macintyre, C. and McVitty, K. (2003) *Planning the Pre-5 Setting*. London: David Fulton.

Macintyre, C. and McVitty, K. (2004) *Movement and Learning in the Early Years*. London: Sage/Paul Chapman.

Adapting the PE Curriculum

Philip Vickerman

Physical education (PE) offers many opportunities for children with coordination difficulties to develop their physical, mental, social, health and general well-being. However, much of the success or otherwise experienced in PE relies heavily on the quality of teaching and learning children receive, combined with an appreciation and commitment to modify and adapt the curriculum to support their specific needs.

In recent years the education sector has experienced an increased emphasis on the inclusion of children with special educational needs (SEN) through legislation such as the National Curriculum (NC) 2000 Statutory Inclusion Statement, the SEN and Disability Rights Act 2001 and the Revised SEN Code of Practice 2001. In addition, the Teacher Training Agency 2002 Professional Standards Framework for the award of Qualified Teacher Status and the Office for Standards in Education Inspection Framework 2002 have increased their focus on the scrutiny of and delivery of PE for children with SEN.

Within this backdrop this chapter sets out to support teachers and schools in establishing key principles and values to consider when planning for the inclusion of children with coordination difficulties in PE. The chapter highlights a range of strategies for adapting the PE curriculum to meet the needs of children in mainstream and special school contexts, while providing a starting point for issues to be considered when planning for children's entitlement and accessibility to physical activity.

Interpreting the PE curriculum

According to the Qualifications and Curriculum Authority (QCA) PE is a 'process of developing pupils' knowledge, skills and understanding so that they can perform reflectively and with increasing physical competence and confidence. This process requires pupils to think as well as perform' (QCA, 1999, p.1). Consequently, PE is concerned with the involvement and development of physical skills, knowledge of the body in action and attitudes to engagement in physical activity. As a result, PE requires children (including those with SEN) to be predominantly physically active in order to improve skilfulness and develop learning in which growing competence leads to personal confidence and increased self-esteem.

In relation to children with coordination difficulties the challenge for schools and teachers is to create a PE curriculum that provides:

> the range of tasks, contexts and environments so that an individual's skills can be tuned, adjusted, adapted, modified and refined. The challenge of teaching is to provide information, ideas and encouragement for each pupil to become competent and confident in each new task, context and environment and then extend them again.
>
> (QCA, 1999, p.1)

Within this context, the PE curriculum is delivered through six activity areas: dance, games, gymnastics, athletics, outdoor and adventurous activities, and swimming and water safety. This broad, balanced and relevant curriculum (Education Reform Act 1988) seeks to provide children with a diverse range of experiences in order to develop and extend their physical and personal development and general well-being.

The PE NC 2000 is divided into four content areas:

- acquiring and developing skills;

- selecting and applying skills, tactics and compositional ideas;

- knowledge and understanding of fitness and health;

- evaluating and improving performance.

These sections, delivered through the six areas of activity, and with recognition of the principles of the Statutory Inclusion Statement (NC 2000) (i.e. setting suitable learning challenges, responding to pupils' diverse learning needs and overcoming potential barriers to learning and assessment) establish the context for the implementation of the PE curriculum in primary, secondary and special schools.

This provision, as part of the NC 2000, should be made available to all children, including those with coordination difficulties, and teachers will need to think in many different ways about what and how they are going to teach, while making best use of their differentiation, teaching and learning strategies. Sugden and Talbot (1998) support this view, suggesting that teaching children with SEN should be seen as an extension of teachers' mixed ability teaching. Thus flexibility of teaching and learning strategies is central to successful inclusive PE. This view is similar to that of Dyson and Millward (2000) and Ainscow et al. (1999) who focus on emphasizing change with teachers and the need to be proactive and adapt the curriculum to meet the individual needs of children with SEN.

Including children with coordination difficulties in PE – some general principles

It is important to acknowledge that as part of an inclusive society, equality of opportunity for pupils in PE is socially and morally right, and schools offer ideal opportunities for all pupils to learn mutual understanding and respect for difference and diversity. In order for teachers of PE to begin to consider planning for inclusion in their lessons, it is essential to first recognize that children have a fundamental right to access the curriculum, which is supported through legislation (i.e. the SEN and Disability Rights Act 2001; NC 2000). However, in interpreting this legislation, schools and teachers should acknowledge that the success factors for including children with coordination difficulties in PE lessons are an open mind, positive attitude and high pupil expectations.

In considering this it is crucial to appreciate this does not mean devising strategies to include all pupils in the same way. In contrast, in order to plan for full access to the PE curriculum teachers need to develop skills in identifying individual children's needs, then begin to plan accordingly for them. Dyson (1999) supports this view, by suggesting that equality of opportunity and inclusiveness should be concerned with celebrating difference, and creating systems in which children are treated equally, but differently, in order to meet their individual needs for accessibility and entitlement to all aspects of the PE curricula and extra curricular programmes.

As a consequence, often the greatest restrictive factor to a barrier-free PE curriculum is not the child with SEN who is being perceived as different, but the lack of flexibility and/or commitment to modify and adapt existing practices on the part of schools, teachers and the other pupils. This view is particularly well emphasized by Fredrickson and Cline (2002) who suggest that 'at one extreme then, the environmentally focused approach holds that there are no children with learning difficulties, only adults with teaching difficulties'. As a result, in order to implement changes to the PE curriculum, Farrell (2001) and Ainscow et al. (1999) advocate that in relation to children with coordination difficulties it may be necessary to consider new ways of involving all pupils, and to draw on skills of experimentation, reflection and collaboration with external agencies and individuals.

Adapting the PE NC 2000 to cater for all pupils' needs

The PE NC 2000 states 'teachers must take action' and 'ensure their pupils are enabled to participate' (QCA, 1999, p. 33), and be responsive to a diverse range of pupil needs in order to facilitate inclusive PE. In meeting this requirement good inclusive planning is central to a child with coordination difficulties gaining access to the curriculum. This involves the development of a teaching and learning pedagogy which meets the statutory requirements to facilitate entitlement, accessibility and inclusion to the PE curriculum. Furthermore, whether a teacher is working in a mainstream or special school, they should consider inclusion as part of their professional practice and not something that is only delivered because there is a statutory requirement to do so.

In reviewing inclusion within the PE curriculum, it is vital that teachers and schools move beyond the level of recognizing the philosophy of inclusion and making superficial changes such as policy statements with no real action to ensuring that they make a difference for pupils in practice. Therefore, in order to have real impact, inclusion should be seen as part of a 'process model' in which all the relevant issues, values and principles are embedded throughout everything teachers do. This involves recognition of the values and philosophy of inclusion, through to the planning, delivery and review of effective inclusive teaching and learning experiences for pupils with coordination difficulties. As a result, Farrell (1998) argues, teachers must be willing to move beyond an acknowledgement of inclusion policies and be prepared 'to reconsider their structure, teaching approaches, pupil grouping and use of support' (1998, p. 81).

Sugden and Talbot (1998) support this view in suggesting that any outcomes in PE for children with coordination difficulties are a result of three interacting variables, namely:

- the resources the individual brings to the activity and or learning situation;

- the context in which learning takes place (teaching and learning);

- the nature of the task to be performed.

This supports the principles noted above in relation to teachers getting to know the individual needs of pupils and adopting flexibility in teaching and learning approaches and a readiness to modify tasks as necessary to ensure successful outcomes for each pupil concerned. Further to Sugden and Talbot's model, the inclusion spectrum (see Fig. 7.1) is another method teachers can adopt in which they move in and out of a range of teaching and learning strategies to ensure access to the PE curriculum for children with coordination difficulties. This model is extensively examined in the DfES (2003) CD-ROM resource *Success For All – An Inclusive Approach to PE and School Sport* (available from dfes@prolog.uk.com). This CD-ROM, produced by the Department for Education and Skills in partnership with the QCA and the English Federation for Disability Sport, has nine case studies of inclusive PE and school sport, evidencing 'real-life' examples of good practice in schools. The resource offers extensive information on teaching and learning strategies, web links and interviews with a range of individuals, schools and pupils involved in inclusive PE. This resource is free and can be ordered from the DfES Publication Centre at the e-mail address above. Each of the case studies features several interviews with teachers, advisory teachers, learning support assistants, physiotherapists, pupils, parents and SEN coordinators in order to support the need for holistic approaches to the development of good practice in inclusion.

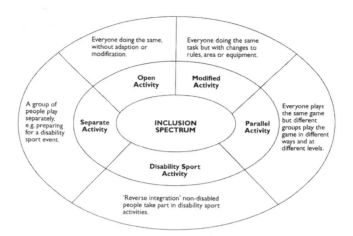

Figure 7.1 The inclusion spectrum.

Reproduced courtesy of the Youth Sport Trust.

Examples of the inclusion spectrum

An example of a Parallel Activity could be in athletics where a child is using a wheelchair to undertake sprinting activities. Consequently, while the majority of the class are working on sprinting technique using their arms, legs and body positioning, the child with SEN would be working on similar principles but with a focus on wheelchair manoeuvrability. These activities can be undertaken within the same learning environment, but with pupils working on different tasks according to their specific needs.

A Modified Activity involves the adaptation of resources or task. For example, a child with coordination difficulties when playing badminton may use a large racquet head, sponge ball or lower net to increase success. The child would then move towards working with a shuttlecock as their skill and confidence levels improve.

Key values to consider in PE

The 1992 PE NC identified four key principles related to equality of opportunity, which still hold true today, to be considered when including children with coordination difficulties. These are entitlement, accessibility, integration and integrity, and are the cornerstones upon which the PE NC 2000 has been revised and extended.

In relation to entitlement, the premise is to acknowledge pupils' fundamental right to be able to access the PE curriculum. This is of particular relevance to children with coordination difficulties with the emergence of the SEN and Disability Rights Act 2001, which gives a fundamental right to inclusive activity, and the revised SEN Code of Practice implemented in January 2002. As part of this entitlement, teachers and schools are expected to take action and plan for inclusive practice in order to facilitate pupils' full entitlement to the PE NC. This shift in legislation recognizes the philosophy of positive attitudes and open minds, and the commitment to recognition of a pupil's right to access PE, in which teachers overcome potential barriers through consultation and the adoption of flexible teaching, learning and assessment strategies.

In terms of accessibility, it is the responsibility of teachers to ensure PE lessons are accessible, barrier-free and relevant to the diversity of pupil needs in their class. This recognizes the social model of disability (see Reiser and Mason, 1990) in which it is a teacher's responsibility to adjust their teaching and learning in order to accommodate the needs of individual children rather than the child being seen as the barrier to participation. An important premise to consider is that often teachers already have the necessary skills to facilitate inclusive PE whatever a pupil's needs may be, and as a result only occasionally will require specialist advice and guidance.

Thus the fundamental factor in successful inclusive activity for all pupils is a positive attitude, good differentiation and a readiness to adapt and modify practices to meet individual needs. For example, a child with dyspraxia who struggles to send and receive a ball in games activities may require specific interventions to increase success and confidence and improve their general motor development. This may require modifications to equipment size (i.e. larger balls or racquet heads), weight, height or texture.

The third principle of integration recognizes the benefits of inclusive education and the positive outcomes that can be achieved for all pupils through such approaches. This also begins to address the government's citizenship agenda in which pupils are educated to have mutual understanding and respect for individual diversity as part of their involvement and participation within a socially inclusive society. PE as a subject area offers many opportunities for children to work cooperatively and value the individual strengths and differences of all pupils concerned.

In relation to the fourth principle of integrity, teachers and schools are expected to underpin their teaching and learning practice by valuing the adaptations and modifications they make in order to plan effectively for the inclusion of children with coordination difficulties. As part of this personal commitment, teachers should ensure inclusive PE is of equal worth, challenging and in no way patronizing or demeaning to the individual child concerned. Thus if teachers deliver activities to children with coordination difficulties that have no educational content or are demeaning and require little contribution in relation to that of other pupils, they are not meeting the requirements of integrity within the PE curriculum.

The PE NC 2000 Statutory Inclusion Statement

As part of any teaching and learning philosophy and practice, it is important that teachers value the four principles from the PE NC 1992 examined above (entitlement, accessibility, integration and integrity). In addition, as part of the revised NC 2000, and in conjunction with the four principles noted earlier, teachers should spend time interpreting the statutory inclusion statement and examine the three statements related to 'setting suitable learning challenges', 'responding to pupils' diverse needs' and 'overcoming potential barriers to learning and assessment for individuals and groups of pupils'.

In relation to setting suitable learning challenges the NC 2000 states: 'Teachers should aim to give every pupil the opportunity to experience success in learning and to achieve as high a standard as is possible' (QCA, 1999, p. 28). It suggests this can be achieved by teaching knowledge, skills and understanding of PE from earlier key stages if appropriate with the aim of ensuring pupils progress and achieve. Therefore, it could be argued inclusion is about focusing upon earlier developmental expectations, or adopting a more flexible teaching approach to accommodate an individual's needs in terms of teaching, learning and assessment. Sugden and Talbot (1998), for example, support this view through the principles of 'moving to learn' and 'learning to move'. They argue: 'Physical education has a distinctive role to play, because it is not simply about education of the physical but involves cognitive, social, language and moral development and responsibilities' (1998, p. 22).

Thus one strategy to facilitate inclusion may involve a shift from the traditional (learning to move) outcome of PE in which skills are taught and learned, to a wider experience of PE (moving to learn) involving opportunities to plan for the social inclusion of pupils across a diverse continuum of learning needs. As a result, it is important to consider the structure and delivery of learning outcomes carefully in order to ensure pupils with coordination difficulties have opportunities to demonstrate a wide variety of movement learning experiences.

'Learning to move' principles can be considered an intrinsic benefit of PE and is the traditional outcome that can be expected from any lesson in which physical skills are taught and learned. Consequently, for a child with general coordination difficulties in gymnastics, it may be necessary to have as a major aim the support and development of fundamental movement patterns such as balance and turns prior to work on more complex activities or sequences.

In relation to moving to learn, outcomes are constructed as a result of the extrinsic experiences of PE, and are not so much concerned with the quality of movement. Thus for a child who has had previous negative experiences and success in PE, it may be necessary for teachers to construct activities that develop and raise self-esteem and confidence in the subject matter. For example, teachers could praise a child's quality of effort, motivation or responses to questions, which in turn raises confidence and a desire to remain on task in the PE lesson.

In relation to responding to pupils' diverse learning needs the NC 2000 states: 'When planning teachers should set high expectations and provide opportunities for all pupils to achieve' (QCA, 1999, p. 29). This section suggests lessons should be planned to ensure full and effective access and that teachers need to be aware of equal opportunity legislation. This begins to address the need to focus on how outcomes can be differentiated and measured for each child, rather than focusing upon philosophical definitions of what equality consists of. A key feature of this occurring will need to be based upon the social model of disability and a commitment to change the activity or teaching and learning style to fit the child rather than the other way round. Thus pupils with SEN should be set appropriate learning outcomes and expectations, while having a variety of opportunities to demonstrate their knowledge and understanding.

This leads into the third statement of overcoming potential barriers to learning and assessment for individuals and groups of pupils in which the PE NC 2000 states 'a minority of pupils will have particular learning and assessment requirements which go beyond the provisions described earlier and if not addressed could create barriers to participation' (QCA, 1999, p. 30). Consequently, as part of the establishment of suitable learning challenges, teachers and schools need in the planning phase to consider how pupils are going to evidence their attainment when it comes to the assessment phase of the lesson. Therefore, adopting a flexible approach to the methods in which pupils are assessed and demonstrate their understanding minimizes the potential for barriers to learning outcomes being achieved. Thus it may be difficult for a child with a coordination difficulty to demonstrate a precise movement skill; however, through a combination of demonstration and verbal description their knowledge, skills and understanding can easily be assessed.

Practical examples of inclusion in practice

When planning for inclusive PE, it is important to start from the premise of full inclusion within the activity, and where this may not be possible, to consider adaptation and or modification of teaching and learning strategies or activities.

A central success factor is initially to consult where appropriate with the pupil and/or relevant professionals and teachers as part of a multi-disciplinary approach. This enables consideration at the planning stage of any differentiation that may be required. This further supports the principles of equality of opportunity and the statutory inclusion statement by acknowledging individual diversity and responding accordingly to pupils' individual needs.

An example of this could be in games activities such as basketball, where pupils may initially require lighter, larger or different coloured balls in order to access the activity. Adaptations to rules may need to be considered such as allowing a player with movement restrictions five seconds to receive and play the ball. In addition, if utilizing such a strategy, it is vital that all members of the group understand the need for such an adaptation in order that they can play to this rule during a game.

In gymnastics or dance, a child with coordination difficulties may require a hand to aid their balance and to provide emotional support if walking along a bench or making rapid turns or twists. This support could be gradually reduced as their movement confidence grows. Another example of inclusive participation in athletics with children with restricted physical movement may involve one push of their wheelchair rather than a jump into the sand pit, or reducing distances to run or travel.

In summary the examples noted above demonstrate how the practice of inclusive PE can be delivered if you are prepared to recognize the key principles and values noted earlier in this chapter. A critical success factor is to adopt flexible approaches to your teaching and learning, and be prepared to try out strategies to see if they work. As part of teachers' developing competence in the area of inclusive PE, they should not be afraid to risk failure in their attempts to create barrier-free lessons – the important point is that teachers learn from their experiences, then try again, rather than restrict themselves to limited teaching and learning strategies.

Summary: facilitating an inclusive approach to your teaching and learning

It is evident from analysis within this chapter that PE for children with coordination difficulties is a key issue for the government, schools and teachers to address in the forthcoming years. The philosophical basis of inclusive PE is socially and morally sound and is supported through legislation and the development of new practices in the PE NC 2000.

Teachers' roles and that of schools are central to the success or failure of the PE inclusion agenda in ensuring that the needs of the many, rather than of the few, are met within the curriculum. In order to consider how to meet this agenda, there is a need to establish a clear and consistent framework for all the key stakeholders involved in inclusive PE to adopt. 'The Eight P's Inclusive PE Framework' (Vickerman, 2002) helps to clarify the widely held views of inclusion being seen as a combination of philosophy, process and practice, and draws together a number of key points considered within this chapter. As a result teachers and schools are encouraged to use this framework as a basis for considering, planning, delivering and reviewing their emerging practice in inclusive PE.

The 'Eight P's Inclusive PE Framework' (Vickerman, 2002) encourages teachers and schools to recognize and spend time analyzing, planning and implementing each of the interrelated factors detailed below in ensuring they give the best opportunities to create barrier-free PE lessons for children with coordination difficulties. The first point is to recognize and embrace the **philosophy** behind inclusion discussed within this chapter as a basic and fundamental human right, which is supported through statutory and non-statutory guidance such as the SEN and Disability Rights Act 2001, the revised Code of Practice and the PE NC Statutory Inclusion Statement 2000.

In order to facilitate this process teachers should embrace a **purposeful** approach to fulfilling the requirements of the PE NC. Consequently, time should be spent examining the philosophical basis of inclusion, while noting the rationale and arguments behind inclusive education. In order to achieve this, a **proactive** approach to the development and implementation of inclusive teaching and learning should be established – as should a readiness to consult actively with fellow teachers, pupils and related individuals and agencies in order to produce a **partnership** approach to delivery.

Inclusion demands a recognition and commitment to modify and adapt teaching and learning styles in order to enable access and entitlement to the PE curriculum, and an obligation to undertake this through a value-based approach. The development of inclusive PE must therefore be recognized as part of a **process** that evolves, emerges and changes over time, and it is important to acknowledge it will require ongoing review by all the key stakeholders.

In conclusion, it is the role of teachers and that of the whole school to ensure inclusion is reflected within **policy** documentation, as a means of monitoring, reviewing and evaluating delivery. The critical success factors, however, rely on ensuring policy impacts on **pedagogical** practices. Thus, while philosophies and processes are vital for schools and teachers, at the end of the day they should ultimately measure success in terms of effective inclusive **practice** which makes a real difference to the experiences pupils with coordination difficulties receive in PE lessons.

Organizations that coordinate sport for people with disabilities

National coordination of international multi-disciplinary competition/activity

- British Paralympic Association (BPA): www.paralympics.org.uk

UK/home country sports associations

- English Federation of Disability Sport (EFDS): www.efds.net

- Disability Sport Cymru: www.sports-council-wales.co.uk/index2.cfm

- Scottish Disability Sport (SDS):http://scottishdisabilitysport.com

- Northern Ireland Committee on Sport for People with Disabilities: www.dsni.co.uk

National disability sports organizations

All the following may be contacted via: www.efds.net

- British Wheelchair Sports Foundation (BWSF): www.britishwheelchairsports.org

- Cerebral Palsy Sport (CP Sport)

- British Amputee and Les Autres Sports Association (BALASA)

- British Blind Sport (BBS)

- British Deaf Sports Council (BDSC)

- English Sports Association for People with a Learning Disability (ESAPLD)

- Disability Sport England

- UK Deaf Sport

National sport-specific disability organizations

For example:

- Great Britain Wheelchair Basketball Association

- Riding for the Disabled

- British Table Tennis Association for the Disabled

- RYA Sailability

The English Federation of Disability Sport

The English Federation of Disability Sport (EFDS) was established in 1998 and is the umbrella organization for disabled sportsmen and women in England.

The EFDS believes that physical education, like sport, is for everyone and that all disabled people have the right to enjoy as wide a range of sporting choices as a matter of common and standard practice.

The EFDS brings together a number of established national and regional agencies with complementary roles. The national agencies listed above each have their own development programmes and are strongly involved in elite level competitive sporting structures, including national and international championships.

The aim of the EFDS is to provide a 'first stop shop' on disability sport issues and to:

- increase the effectiveness of the structure of disability sport;

- promote the inclusion of disabled people within mainstream programmes of national governing bodies of sport, local authorities and other providers;

- raise the profile of sport for disabled people.

The EFDS also has nine regional offices with varying staffing structures but at least a Regional Development Manager employed in each region. Details of the National Disability Sport Organizations are available from EFDS Head Office:

English Federation of Disability Sport
Manchester Metropolitan University
Alsager Campus
Hassall Road, Alsager
Stoke on Trent
ST7 2HL

Tel: 0161 247 5294
Fax: 0161 247 6895
E-mail: federation@efds.co.uk
Website: www.efds.co.uk
Minicom: 0161 247 5644

Youth Sport Trust

The Youth Sport Trust is a charity established in 1994 to effect change and to build a brighter future for young people in sport.

The Trust is achieving this by:

- promoting the benefit of physical education and sport for young people;

- delivering TOP programmes – a series of structured, linked and progressive opportunities for young people (see below);

- providing training – for teachers, leaders, coaches and parents;

- developing resources – for teachers, sports development officers, PE professionals, sports leaders and coaches;

- offering information and advice – for national and local agencies in youth sport.

Inclusion in the TOP programmes

Ensuring the inclusion of young disabled people is a key priority of the TOP programmes delivered by the Youth Sport Trust. Below is a brief résumé of the programmes showing the inclusion aspects:

TOP Tots	Constructive play activities aimed at parents and carers of children 18 months to three years of age.
Inclusion	Specific information in the TOP Tots booklet.

TOP start	Pre-school and nursery activity programme for children aged three to five years.
Inclusion	Resource card and some specific equipment items.

TOP Play	Core skills and fun sport for four to nine years olds.
Inclusion	Specific equipment items in the TOP Play bag; ideas in the 'Including Young Disabled People' handbook; positive images throughout all the cards

BT TOP Sport	Introduces specific sports to 7 to 11 year olds:
	basketball – cricket – football – hockey – netball – rugby – squash – swimming – table tennis – tennis – hurling/camogie (Northern Ireland).
Inclusion	Resource cards giving sports-specific ideas on each sport; additional ideas in the 'Including Young Disabled People' handbook; positive images throughout all the cards.

TOP Athletics	Introduces athletics to 7 to 11 year olds.
Inclusion	Double-sided resource card; positive images and ideas throughout all the cards; inclusion section in the handbook.

TOP Gymnastics	Introduces gymnastics to 4 to 11 year olds.
Inclusion	Five specific resource cards mirroring the main themes; inclusion section in the handbook.

Ecclesiastical Insurance TOP Link	Seeks to develop leadership opportunities for young people in Key Stage 3 and 4 along with closer staff–pupil links between secondary and feeder primaries.
Inclusion	Includes leadership training programme for young people in special education; encourages the inclusion of special schools in festivals.

Sportsability	Inclusive games programme with specific equipment, resource material and training in boccia, goal ball, polybat, table cricket and table hockey. Provides unique, innovative equipment and 16 activity-specific resource cards.

Specialist Sports Colleges	Encourages maintained secondary schools in England to apply for designation as sports colleges.
Inclusion	Working with school and community partners to encourage the inclusion of all young people in SSC programmes; specific inclusion training available.

TOP Outdoors	Helps teachers develop outdoor and adventurous activities with their pupils.
Inclusion	Two double-sided resource cards and section in handbook.

New Programme	A Project Group has been developing resource material and examples of good practice when including young people who have profound and multiple impairments in physical activity programmes.

Scheme Trainer Training	Basic ideas on inclusion defined by National Trainers at YST national scheme trainer training.

Inclusive Activities Workshops	One-day course on inclusion for TOPs for Scheme Trainers (Curriculum and Community) delivered by YST National staff. Schemes bid for one of six course dates per year (or by arrangement).

TOP Up Ability	Top Up Ability
Four-hour workshop on inclusion for TOPs for teachers (funded by Coaching for Teachers).	Three-hour workshop on inclusion for TOPs for community deliverers (must be self-funded by scheme).

Training – Sportsability

The model illustrated in Fig. 7.2 shows how the National Sportsability training programme operates. The model offers cascade training through a network of accredited national and local trainers to ensure consistency of approach and delivery. At a local level accredited trainers through arrangement with the Youth Sport Trust deliver courses for individuals on how to implement the scheme.

Trainer training

- One-day workshop (six hours) delivered by two National Trainers.

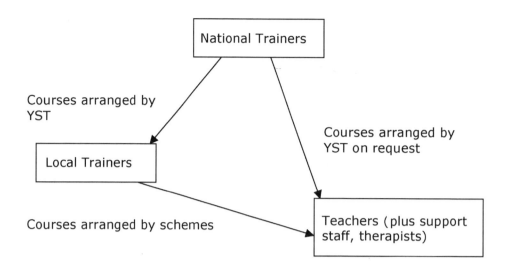

Figure 7.2 National Sportsability training programme.

Local or national training of teachers

■ Four-hour workshop delivered by local trainer(s) or one National Trainer.

Basic information on the TOP programmes is contained in the leaflet *Bringing Sport to Life for Young People*. Updates are available from the Youth Sport Trust via newsletters and information sheets, e.g. *TOPs* and *Ink Clued*.

For more information on the Youth Sport Trust's inclusion programmes contact:

Youth Sport Trust
Rutland Building
Loughborough University
Loughborough
LE11 3TU

Tel: 01509 226600
Fax: 01509 210851

Working in Collaboration with the Therapist

Lois Addy

The identification and remediation of developmental coordination disorder (DCD) has, for many years, been reliant on the expertise of a number of health professionals, namely occupational therapists, physiotherapists and speech and language therapists. Each professional was able to draw on his/her professional knowledge in order to provide a comprehensive understanding of the specific needs of the child with DCD, often contributing to diagnosis and inevitably therapeutic intervention. The initial education of each professional provided differing perspectives on the child's needs and how these could be met, and although this expertise is still valid, its implementation has changed and adapted as educational inclusion has gained in momentum.

To qualify and practise, **occupational therapists** are required to have a comprehensive understanding of anatomy and physiology, neurology and psychology in order to be able to identify possible functional difficulties experienced by individuals with a range of disorders. Remediation involves the identification of dysfunctional skills through observation and activity analysis, and the implementation of carefully graded activities which have meaning to the individual, to develop new or relearn old skills in order to optimize independence. The combined appreciation of child development, neurology and child and cognitive psychology has provided paediatric occupational therapists with a comprehensive understanding of fine/gross motor and perceptual development. These skills in particular have led to the occupational therapist being a lead professional in the diagnosis and remediation of children with DCD. Indeed children with DCD account for on average 30.4 per cent of the number of children seen by paediatric occupational therapists (NAPOT, 2003).

Physiotherapists are required to have an extensive knowledge of anatomy and physiology, and are experts in analysing movement difficulties. According to the Chartered Society of Physiotherapy, the profession emphasizes the examination of 'movement based on the structure and function of the body and uses physical approaches to promote health, and prevent, treat and manage disease and disability'. Physiotherapy aims at improving the quality of movement with both the planning and carrying out of movements in children with DCD. This is achieved through exercises, games and activities.

The education of **speech and language therapists** includes a balance of both theoretical and practical components relating to language pathology and therapeutics, speech and language sciences, behavioural sciences, biomedical sciences, education, acoustics and some psychology, the aim being to enable people to communicate to the best of their ability. Most speech and language therapists work in NHS hospitals or clinics, but some are directly employed by an education authority to work within schools.

Speech and language therapists have an essential role in helping children with oral dyspraxia. This is demonstrated in the reduced ability to voluntarily control single or sequenced silent movements of the lips, tongue or soft palate, in a similar way to children with DCD who have difficulties in planning and organizing certain fine and gross motor movements. It is an extremely frustrating condition, as the child knows what he wants to say but persistently makes speech errors which are not usually made at his age. Sometimes the child may be able to pronounce a sentence spontaneously but when asked to repeat this cannot coordinate the muscles to sound out the words. Speech may be very difficult to understand as the child struggles to produce single speech sounds. This obviously has an enormous effect on the child's self-esteem and self-confidence.

Delivering therapy for children with DCD

Exactly how therapists work with children with DCD has changed enormously over the last decade with the inclusion movement being influential in challenging traditional practices. The health science-led education of professions allied to medicine has equipped each professional with an insight into the biological, neurological and psychological processes which may be impaired in children with DCD. But the focus offered by each therapist has differed according to his or her professional training and subsequent experience. Sadly this led to a compartmentalized approach whereby physiotherapy would focus on the child's poor gross motor coordination, movement and balance; occupational therapy would consider poor fine motor control and its particular effect on handwriting, in addition to the effects of distorted perceptual and sensory integration on the child's functional performance; and speech and language therapy would address the complex difficulties presented by children with oral dyspraxia.

School-based therapy provision

The approach outlined above frequently involved children being withdrawn from school to attend therapy sessions based at child development centres or clinics. Such therapist-directed attendance with advice being sent into school via parent reports or occasional consultation visits was economical in relation to therapy resources but dissatisfying in respect to continuity, consistency and integration of skills within the education and home environment.

As the inclusion movement has increased in its momentum, so too have therapeutic practices changed to meet the individual needs of children in the context where they learn. Therefore increasingly therapists, particularly occupational therapists, now work with children within the school or home, and only in specific circumstances are children withdrawn from school to attend a child development centre or clinic. These occasions involve detailed assessments which are perhaps impossible to carry out in the school setting, or the provision of specialized therapy such as sensory integration which requires the use of a specifically designed room containing equipment such as swings, bolsters, soft matting, etc.

The continued desire to address the child's needs within his learning environment has led to therapists increasingly sharing their practice with teachers and integrating therapy goals with curriculum objectives. This has the positive effect that 'therapeutic intervention is delivered in a holistic manner and blended with a functional activity for the child, rather than leading to compartmentalising parts of a child's body or daily life, according to which professional discipline is involved at any one time' (Mackey and McQueen, 1998).

The inclusion of children with DCD has provided therapists with a shift in thinking which has caused a move away from adopting a multidisciplinary approach where each professional acts independently towards interdisciplinary methods where there is partial collaboration between qualified practitioners. Ultimately there is a need to strive towards transdisciplinary practice whereby different disciplines are integrated to provide a unified approach. It is only through understanding and respecting the varying professional perspectives that true transdisciplinary collaboration can occur.

The move towards this transdisciplinary thinking has not been without its tensions, as health-based therapy resources remain limited despite the increased numbers of children with DCD requiring help. Today therapists will receive requests for help from a variety of sources for vast numbers of children with DCD (NAPOT, 2003). As the number of children referred for therapy is high, this has caused therapists to consider various methods of integrating therapy and education which aim to address the child's needs within the constraints of their staffing resources (McWilliams, 1995). These range from consultation through to working with the child in the classroom with the whole class involved.

A consultation approach is commonly used due to restrictions in staffing resources. This involves the therapist identifying the specific needs of the child through detailed assessment of the child's functioning skills in a variety of settings. For example, a typical paediatric occupational therapist assessment would include: examination of the child's gross motor coordination and balance during a PE lesson, interviews with teachers, parents and the child himself, the use of standardized measures to identify specific perceptual difficulties such as the non-motor Test of Visual Motor Integration (Beery and Buktenica, 2004), and the Non-Motor Test of Visual Perceptual Skills Revised (Gardner, 1996), along with the Movement Assessment Battery for Children (Henderson and Sugden, 1992). An analysis of handwriting would also be included. In addition the child's sensory profile and kinaesthetic abilities may be analysed. At the end of this comprehensive evaluation the teacher would be consulted regarding the assessment results and a programme of activities and classroom adaptations would be recommended which may or may not align with the expectations of the National Curriculum.

This approach is useful in establishing therapeutic routines that sustain the child's functional performance in the classroom (Dunn, 1991). However, its value in terms of inclusion could be questioned. There appears an imbalance in the shift of power between the therapist and teacher. The therapists are frequently viewed as the 'expert' and the rich debate enjoyed through shared problem-solving and collaboration can be limited by time constraints.

Training school staff

One effective way of using consultation is the use of **pupil presentations**. Once the therapist has acquired a comprehensive appreciation of the child's specific needs, a forum can be held whereby *all* teaching staff, support assistants, parent helpers and school support workers, such as dinner ladies, across year groups can meet. The therapist can use this meeting, with the child and his parent's permission, to describe the child's needs, provide some understanding as to *why* the child may have the needs, and offer some solutions to the difficulties in terms of specific programmes, classroom strategies, adaptations, language use and social integration. Often by raising awareness of how the child is actually 'perceiving his world', tremendous insight and empathy can be gained which can have the benefit of providing a consistent approach to enabling the child achieve his potential. Training sessions such as these can be arranged with the child's therapists and planned into Inset days or staff meetings after school. The choice of health professional depends on the precise need of the child. For example, should the child's gross motor control and balance be of great concern affecting PE and social inclusion, the physiotherapist may be the most appropriate person to invite. When the child is struggling with classroom activities, handwriting, peer-relationships and PE, the occupational therapist may be the most appropriate professional to invite.

Physiotherapists, occupational therapists and speech and language therapists will often provide therapy within school but withdraw the child with DCD from the classroom into an adjacent room. This is known as **individual pull-out** or direct service therapy (McWilliams, 1995). Therapy focus is directly and exclusively on the child's functioning, usually on the area of greatest need. This approach might be used by the occupational therapist to focus on developing the child's handwriting or dysfunctional perception which are impacting on certain aspects of the child's learning such as construction, reading and art. Alternatively the focus may be on developing gross motor skills, focusing on those required to participate effectively in PE. This approach relies on the therapist travelling to the school at a time convenient to the school. Usually only one session per week is provided with follow-up activities being given to the child's teacher to continue as time allows. This approach has the benefit of both therapist and teacher being involved with the child's needs with sharing of concerns being commonplace. However, given the restrictions in time available, continuity and consistency can be limited and at times it can feel similar to the limitations involved in 'having a piano lesson without having a piano to practise on'.

The advantage of pull-out therapy, according to Bundy (1991), is that pupils will refine one or more of the skills associated with success in the school, i.e. fine motor skills, postural adaptations and handwriting/keyboarding skills. It also helps to develop an engaged therapeutic relationship with the child so that both the psychological and physical needs of the child can be addressed. This allows the therapist to carefully monitor the child's self-esteem, which is known to be vulnerable in children with DCD.

Group intervention

Another method used to integrate therapy is **small group pull-out**. In certain situations, when the child may be at risk of being stigmatised for being withdrawn from class to receive therapy or where a group ethos is required, a small group of children are selected to attend a therapy group provided by the occupational therapist, physiotherapist or speech and language therapist within school but outwith the classroom. The teacher, along with the therapist, collaborates in selecting peers who would also benefit from receiving specific therapeutic techniques or who could facilitate and encourage a positive reaction from the child with identified needs without it being detrimental to their learning.

There are several programmes established for children with DCD where this is extremely appropriate. Legibility of handwriting is a concern for almost all children with DCD and although guidance can be given by an occupational therapist on a one-to-one basis, this close observation and guidance can apply even more pressure and stress to some children. Therefore there are occasions when handwriting groups may be preferable. Many schools use the 'Write from the Start' perceptuo-motor handwriting programme (Teodorescu and Addy, 1996). This programme guides the child through the fine motor and perceptual processes required to produce legible handwriting. In addition to graphic exercises, the programme also includes related games and activities which lend themselves to a small group. The Speed-up kinaesthetic handwriting programme (Addy, 2004) can be used effectively with an individual child when problems of speed and fluency are affecting the child's handwriting. However, this eight-week programme was intended to be used with a small group of three to four children. This encourages mutual support as well as protected gentle competition outwith the demands and expectations of the rest of the class.

In addition to handwriting, small pull-out groups have been used by occupational therapists to address the social skills of children with DCD along with some of their peers. It is recognized that children with DCD often have poor social skills due to poor body image, distorted self-image, low self-esteem and lack of confidence. However, these skills are often neglected leaving the child vulnerable, isolated and at risk of being bullied or getting into trouble (Losse et al., 1991; Portwood, 2000). Social skills are 'generally acceptable levels of behaviours that enable a person to interact effectively with others and avoid socially unacceptable responses from others' (Gresham and Elliott, 1984, p. 127) therefore it would seem essential that these are addressed within a group situation. The importance of enhancing social skills has been highlighted by the introduction of citizenship to the secondary curriculum in 2002 and primary curriculum in 2003 with the premise that 'education is about helping pupils to develop the knowledge, skills and understanding they need to live confident, healthy, independent lives, as individuals, parents, workers and members of society' (DfEE/QCA, 1999). Occupational therapists are able to facilitate a social skills programme under the auspices of citizenship or personal development time. Activities, role-play and drama are used successfully to teach skills which are then practised and reinforced in the classroom (Dixon and Addy, 2004). In addition, selected activities can be recommended for use in class circle time. This can provide the confidence and secure environment that the child with DCD needs to share concerns.

Classroom support

In certain situations therapy, in particular occupational therapy and occasionally speech and language therapy, is provided in the classroom on a one-to-one basis. This is often apart from other children but the therapist will operate as if he/she is an additional teacher in the class. Therapy focus is directed towards the area of greatest need, and more often than not this is related to the child's handwriting or perceptual skills linking to organization and recording information. This often will use a 'process-orientated approach', which may contrast to direct teaching approaches. When using this approach the therapist will consider the underlying skills required to develop a single skill, and will use activities to target these rather than adopt a practice/rehearsal method. For example, if a child is struggling to form the individual letter shapes when writing, the therapist will identify whether the child has difficulties in developing form constancy; fine motor skills will be observed, as will the child's hand-eye coordination. The therapist will also identify whether the child has difficulties appreciating different shapes due to being distracted by other nearby forms (figure-ground discrimination). After identifying how the child is perceiving various shapes, the occupational therapist will select a variety of multi-sensory games and activities which will help the child to recognize various simple shapes, i.e. drawing round stencils, creating 3-D shapes out of dough or putty, drawing large shapes on the blackboard, creating forms in sand trays and ultimately drawing individual shapes on paper.

The advantage of using such an approach is that the choice of activities will enhance not only the specific abilities, but also similar skills which can be generalized into a variety of situations. For example, improvements will not only be seen in letter formation but also in the production of shapes in art, practical maths, science and construction. Having the therapist in the classroom enables the teacher to appreciate therapeutic goals and implement similar activities with children with similar needs. In return, the therapist develops a growing awareness of curricular expectations and can theme activities according to the subjects being studied over that period.

Whole-class intervention

A further method of working with children with DCD involves **the whole class** or small/large group. In America, this is familiar practice, and in the UK it is developing in areas where resources are less stretched. This approach sees the occupational therapist or physiotherapist working with the whole class in collaboration with the teacher. Therapy is focused on all children but the emphasis is on meeting the needs of one or more children. It is particularly useful in physical education where there may be a few children with perceptual and motor difficulties requiring assistance in motor coordination, movement and balance. The session may be planned with the teacher and run by the therapist. The activities will be chosen based on kinaesthetic regulation, psychomotor therapy and motor learning, and although targeted at the child/ren with specific needs, will also extend the skills of children without overt motor difficulties. Using this approach it is then possible for the teacher to observe or watch the group and to participate in the planning of the activity.

The use of an occupational therapist to lead the whole class in a handwriting practice session is also a workable option, and has the benefit that the children diagnosed with DCD are not stigmatized or isolated by doing activities which differ to those of their peers.

The ultimate goal of most occupational therapists, physiotherapists and speech and language therapists is to have enough time and resources to help individuals with DCD **during their routine activities**. Ideally therapy would be provided in the location where the greatest need is identified, be this the classroom, home or community. As DCD commonly affects the child's ability to learn, therapy should, ideally, be provided within school and therapeutic activities aligned to National Curriculum objectives. There are occasions when it is possible to implement this approach more than others, for example dressing and undressing before PE/swimming. It is recognized that many children with DCD struggle with their sense of position in space and body awareness, while at the same time have organizational and planning difficulties. This can lead to the child being extremely slow to dress independently. Guidance in this area will often occur at home, but this does not disclose the stressful realities of undressing for PE within a certain time in a common peer group. In these circumstances the occupational therapist can provide subtle direction and guidance immediately prior to the PE lesson, providing the reassurance and affirmation the child requires to succeed. They may also provide adaptations to clothing to compensate for poor motor coordination. Occupational therapy is therefore directly, but not exclusively, focused on the child with DCD. It is useful in that the teacher is involved in observing the therapist's interactions with the child.

Teachers and therapists in collaboration

Increasingly occupational therapists, physiotherapists and speech and language therapists work in collaboration with teachers to enable children with DCD fully to access the educational and social curriculum. The word collaborative is very appropriate as it arises from Latin derivatives 'com' and 'laborare' meaning 'labour together', which implies that it is an interactive process whereby individuals with a range of expertise and varied life experiences can join together in a spirit of willingness to share resources, responsibility and rewards in creating inclusive and effective educational programmes and environments for children with DCD (Rainforth and York-Barr, 1997).

The exciting part about true collaboration is that educators and therapists must work together as equal partners to provide learning opportunities for children with DCD. This requires professionals to become 'learners as well as specialists' (Mackey and McQueen, 1998). Effective use of collaboration is seen when the occupational therapist, physiotherapist or speech and language therapist attends educational planning meetings, takes an active part in the planning of educational programmes and offers suggestions for activities which could be absorbed into classroom routines and would help improve motor learning or perception in a child with DCD without being detrimental to the rest of the class. This allows for the development of mutual respect and a forum for problem-solving. Many services have encouraged active collaboration by allocating a specific-named occupational therapist, physiotherapist or speech and language therapist to the school.

Treatment delivered at a health care base

Although therapists are increasingly working within the school environment, there are situations when it is more appropriate to see the child outside school. There are three occasions when this is appropriate: for the use of standardized assessments; for the provision of specialized interventions; and for the effective and economical use of limited resources.

Use of standardized assessments

All of the therapy professionals working with children with DCD will use specific assessments to identify the exact nature of the child's difficulty. Although all will observe the child within their natural environment, be this at home or at school, there may also be the need to obtain a detailed analysis of certain skills. The paediatric occupational therapist or physiotherapist will use several perceptual assessments which will determine whether certain aspects of the child's development is being affected by impaired visual memory for example, or whether the child is confused by too much visual stimulus (figure-ground discrimination). They will assess the child's sensory processing using, for example, the Sensory Profile (Dunn, 1999) or Sensory Integration Praxis Test (SIPT) (Ayres, 1989). In addition, assessment of fine and gross motor skills will include the use of the Bruininks-Oseretsky Test of Motor Proficiency (Bruininks, 1978) or the Movement ABC (Henderson and Sugden, 1992). These assessments are preferably undertaken in an environment conducive to the requirements of each test, the school setting rarely constituting an appropriate location.

The environment whereby speech and language therapy is offered is crucial and given the sensitive nature of the child's difficulties, pull-out or clinic-based services are often preferred not only by the therapist but also by the child.

Provision of specialised interventions

One key example of an intervention which is perhaps not so conducive to classroom practice is sensory integration. This is a specialized technique used by occupational therapists and physiotherapists working with children with DCD. It is based on the theories of Dr Jean Ayres, an American occupational therapist who believed that many children with DCD have difficulties processing and interpreting the sensory experiences of the body, causing poor regulation of touch, movement, vision, smell, taste, balance and hearing. This results in over- or under-sensitivity to touch, inadequate pressure regulation and poor coordination. It is based on the premis that our bodies naturally crave a state of physiological equilibrium whereby we 'feel comfortable' and are in 'control' of our actions; this is why we get uncomfortable when we are too hot and actively try to regulate our body temperature by removing items of clothing or switching on air conditioning. Children with sensory integration dysfunction yearn to integrate the senses in a more meaningful way, therefore if they have a reduced awareness of limb pressure which causes poor coordination, they subconsciously crave this stimulation and gain it through crashing, bumping and squashing actions.

Sensory integration requires the specific use of selected equipment such as swings, scooter boards, bolsters, air workers, cooperblankets and bodysox, to name but a few, to provide sensory experiences beneficial to each child. The therapist guides the child into exploring the carefully structured environment in order to experience the varied sensory experiences through controlled but child-led play. This may involve swinging, rolling, brushing, tumbling, stroking or compressing according to the child's sensory needs. Through this the child becomes a more efficient organizer of sensory information (Wilson and Kaplan, 1994; Allen and Donald, 1995; Leemrijse et al., 2000).

Although sensory integration is an intervention favoured by many occupational therapists, it is an expensive intervention requiring the therapist to complete postgraduate training and the creation of a therapy room whereby sensory integration can be practised. Interestingly, as the effectiveness of this approach has been questioned (Vargas and Camilli, 1999; Mulligan, 2003), therapists have increasingly considered the extension of this approach into the school environment in the form of a 'sensory diet' (Nackley, 2001). A sensory diet includes a combination of alerting, organizing and calming techniques that lead directly to the development of the 'near' senses (Kranowitz, 1998; Winter and Winter, 2003). This may require the child to have, for example, exercise breaks to improve attention, elastic bands to stretch repeatedly before performing a fine motor task and paper clips to fiddle with in order to help concentration while listening. The combination of sensory integration in addition to the inclusion of a sensory diet and perceptual activities to the child's school day appears to be more effective than therapy provided in isolation (Vargas and Camilli, 1999).

Effective and economical use of limited resources

The third method of providing therapy for children with DCD outside the school environment is the creation of skills-based groups. Therapists typically run these after school. This is an economical use of the therapist's time when professional resources are short.

A group of children with DCD are brought together to address specific dysfunctional skills. For example, the BCB club (balance, coordination and body awareness) was established to address the perceptual and motor needs of a group of children with DCD from across a region of North Yorkshire (Addy, 1996). As the group took place after school, the children's parents and teachers were invited to observe, and the session plan from each group was sent into school to feed back the activities used and describe their purpose. Some teachers used these session plans to run the class PE lesson, encouraging the child who had attended to help when explaining the activities to the rest of the class. The actions were based on motor learning, kinaesthetic training and sensori-motor approaches. Similar session plans have been extended and overtly linked to the National Curriculum objectives for PE, thus ensuring the assimilation of therapy and education (Addy, in press).

Conclusion

In conclusion, it can be seen that there are various methods used by occupational therapists, physiotherapists and speech and language therapists to address the unique needs of children with DCD, which increasingly involve the combination of therapy and education. By integrating the child's therapy into school, interruptions to lessons are virtually eliminated; children do not 'miss out' on the fun activities by being withdrawn from the classroom and subsequently do not fall behind in work. There is also a growing awareness that 'if routine therapy were to be cross-referenced with the National Curriculum it has the potential to reduce the pressure on pupil time, curriculum content and therapy resources' (Mackey and McQueen, 1998). However, the number of paediatric therapists available remains low, which causes considerable frustration for teachers, parents, children and therapists alike. The therapist wants to provide the best service despite limited time and personnel. However, the descriptions provided will enable teachers to determine the range of therapy available to children with DCD along with the various models used, and with this knowledge to engage in shared goal planning in order to maximize the potential of each child with DCD.

A Parent's Perspective

Diane Jenkins

This chapter has been written by Diane Jenkins, a parent of a child who has been diagnosed with dyspraxia. The chapter reflects her experiences of having a child with dyspraxia. It also provides an overview of how a group of local parents went about setting up a parents group for children with coordination difficulties.

Early years

I am the mother of a 12-year-old son, Dale. Dale is dyspraxic. He was born in July 1992 with a very quick delivery but no complications, a much wanted first child for my husband and I. Difficulties arose immediately at the hospital, with Dale being unable to feed properly and scoring low on paediatric checks, but nothing really alarming so no cause for concern. We spoke to our health visitor as Dale scraped through all development checks. Something appeared to be different about Dale. He was slow to sit up, but as he was an only child at that time, hours were spent steadying him into position. Crawling and walking were slow too but because he could talk at a young age he just sat, pointed and recited the words he knew. I'm still convinced he was trying to distract us from his lack of mobility. His high intelligence convinced us as parents, and I believe health visitors, of the problems he had and by the time he started nursery school aged three he could read about 15 words. Although his coordination was poor, there was something different about Dale...

Starting school

I expressed my concerns about his general coordination to his nursery teacher who assured me she would keep an eye on his progress. She agreed with me that he did fall over a lot and often dropped things but he was the youngest in the class and new to school routine. At a parents' evening she showed me a barely recognizable picture Dale had drawn of the tricycles in the yard, which he had chosen as his favourite toy. 'How strange,' I said, 'he cannot pedal his trike at home,' remembering the back-breaking effort of pushing him along while trying to hold his feet on the pedals as they flayed wildly at each side. On further inspections the teacher noticed that each playtime Dale would sit in the back passenger seat on the double trike and wait for another child to come along and pedal him around. There was something different about Dale…

As Reception class loomed, his difficulties really became apparent. Simply getting to school by 9 am, even when getting up at 6.30 am was going to be a major task. I now had another child and the baby had to be fed, so months before his start date we would practise with Dale eating breakfast totally unaided. He had found difficulty in using cutlery and often had to be helped before his meal hit the kitchen floor. Dressing was also rehearsed so that he could manage after PE lessons. These months brought no improvement in skills whatsoever. So along I went again and explained to his new Reception teacher his unexplainable lack of coordination. Mornings were a nightmare, his clothes were laid out carefully on the bed yet he would still manage to get his pants outside of his trousers. We prepared packed lunches to bypass the cutlery situation for lunchtime assistance, yet he would pass the cloakroom where his lunch box was stored and still arrive at the dinner hall without his food on a daily basis. His teacher reported that he did well in his first PE lesson but after that week he got it horribly wrong. He found it impossible to jump with both feet let alone attempt to climb and roll. This was typical of the lack of consistency in his basic skills we had experienced right throughout his early life. Things he could achieve one day he would forget the next.

As he moved up to Year One there were concerns about his letter formation and pencil grip. He had showed no improvement from early Reception days. My husband and I would spend night after night going over handwriting exercises, even taking them in to school to prove the effort we were making, but still no improvement. He charmed all the teachers and older children with his happy disposition and mature sense of humour but didn't seem to mix well with children in his class. There was something different about Dale…

Most of the little boys in his class joined the local football club but when Dale kicked a ball with his right foot his arm would curl upward and he usually fell backwards. Dale had always needed routine: the same bedtime stories, the same things to eat, the same clothes to wear. This became more apparent when I would sometimes turn up at school to pick him up and offer to take him to his favourite park with a picnic tea or swimming with friends. These were treats I knew he liked but he would become very agitated and ask to go home first. After going to sit in his room for a short while and thinking about it for 15 minutes or so he would return and agree to go. This nonconformity led to the first cases of bullying. He was different – we knew it, he felt it and other children sensed it. Being what we regard as fairly laid-back parents, we are not prone to comparison, but our daughter who was two years younger was now achieving things Dale could not. Our visits to our GP, talks to health visitors and visits to family health clinics were all in vain. There was something different about Dale but no one could put their finger on it. We began to feel that professionals thought we were either neurotic or lacking in disciplinary boundaries. His school work was now being corrected or asked to be redone and he would become frustrated and angry. Peers at school began to notice his inadequacies and make fun of him. While the content was very good, Dale's presentation was dreadful.

He was suddenly desperate to ride his two-wheeler bike which had stood in the garage all summer and had caused many a frustrated tantrum when we had tried to use it. We went along to a quiet beach where the sand was hard and he felt confident he wouldn't get hurt when he fell off. On the Sunday of week one and hour four he finally got it. YES!! So we returned on Saturday of week two – he had forgotten!! We spent four hours each consecutive weekend until we cracked it. Whoever coined the phrase 'as easy as riding a bike' never had a dyspraxic child. We tried lots of different activities that may have helped his ever increasing awkwardness. Gymnastics were a joke and he eventually learned to swim quite well, but made it look extremely difficult and continually failed badge assessment because of his technique. My husband and I now felt that when we explained his difficulties some people felt we were making excuses for our child's bad behaviour. But if we didn't try and explain we looked like parents who spent little time encouraging our son to achieve. I reached my lowest ebb when one day he asked me, 'Mum, am I odd?'

Dyspraxia the label

He then moved to Year Two and I again approached his teacher to try and explain his problems. She had recently been on some training and asked me to take Dale back to the GP. Our GP mentioned the word *dyspraxia*, I wrote it down and took it back to his class teacher. She said this is what she had suspected. We were devastated. Could this be cured? Would he grow out of it? Was there medication to eradicate it? There was definitely something different about Dale... I needed to find as much information as I could. I trawled bookshops, surfed the Net, could have opened a library of my own. Everything I read felt as if the author had spent a week in our home. They were talking about our son.

I didn't really want to give my son a label, but this label helped me to explain his problems to him and to others and the more I educated myself the more able I became in helping Dale to recognize and overcome some of his difficulties. Dale finally got help from an occupational therapist and his gross motor skills improved tremendously. His therapist filmed him when he first started and when he was discharged. The improvement was immense. Dale got extra time with his SATS and did extremely well. I could now explain to my child that he wasn't different he was *dyspraxic*. From this point his self-esteem and confidence increased. He was proud to help take care of some baby chicks that were being hand reared in the classroom, but guess who dropped one of the chicks! He retold us the nightmare tale after school one evening but assured us the chick was fine. The next day however, one of the chicks appeared to have a bad wing. 'Miss said it wasn't the one I dropped, Mum', he quoted, 'but I think it was the one that mine landed on'. There is something different about Dale...

Secondary school

Dale started secondary school and this brought a whole new set of problems to deal with. But we planned ahead, liaised with the school beforehand and tried to anticipate what we thought would be problematic. It hasn't been a bed of roses, bullying still being his biggest problem, although he has made several new friends. He is coping well with the work but has to be reminded constantly of his homework and tasks. Multiple instructions are impossible for him, but as he gets older he is developing his own coping strategies. His biggest difficulty is that while he relates well to teachers and older pupils, he does not communicate at all well with boys of his own age. I know we will continue to face problems, but with training and sharing with other parents I know we can help Dale through this.

We gave up on the gymnastics and trying to kick a goal but still encouraged Dale to swim regularly. He has discovered a talent for drama and has become rather successful, taking major roles in many productions and even gaining a small part in a TV drama. When these children find something they can do, they do it really well.

There is something different about Dale, he's dyspraxic, but we wouldn't change him for the world.

Setting up a parent group

'Do you have a child or family member who is dyspraxic?'

The words jumped out at me from the local paper. 'Yes, yes, but I thought I was the only one!' I remember thinking to myself. I contacted the number and spoke to a mum, just like me, who thought she was the only one with a dyspraxic son too. That telephone call lasted an hour as we compared heartaches and even shared tears at the struggles we had experienced in just getting to understand our children's difficulties. Eight people responded to that newspaper piece and a meeting was arranged for everyone to get together.

That first meeting was inspirational, each parent recalling struggles in their child's development, some differing from others but all following a strangely familiar thread, the group consensus being 'we thought it was only our child, and now we know it's not'. We decided to call ourselves the 'Dyspraxia and Associated Difficulties Support Group'.

The group met monthly on a weekday afternoon initially, but as attendance grew, demand meant that evening meetings had to be arranged to accommodate the numbers who were unable to attend during the day. As the group met more regularly it was decided that the meetings should move away from being a sounding board for frustration and despair for lack of public understanding, although this was always needed, and should progress and have clear objectives. While our meeting venue and refreshments were paid from donations from those who attended we were considering something more permanent being established. We contacted our local Voluntary Organizations Bureau who helped us set out a constitution and form a committee so that we could apply for funding for specific projects. A new venue was found at the offices of a charitable organization which gave us a room free of charge. We held awareness seminars with guest speakers, set up an information library where members could borrow books and factsheets on DCD/dyspraxia and were contacted by the Special Educational Needs Department of the local education authority. The advisory teacher from the department arranged to come along to some of our meetings and keep us up to date with what was happening in local schools to benefit children with dyspraxia. Monthly newsletters were produced after each meeting to inform those who were unable to attend about what had gone on.

A large number of parents have contacted the group, some attending meetings regularly, others just giving committee members a ring from time to time, but all finding some comfort from the support of others in the same situation. More recently the group funded an 'away day' to an outdoor pursuits centre for our children. Because of the difference in ages a variety of activities were on offer and every child took part, the finale being a mud assault course. The centre was given a detailed description of the type of difficulties that the children had, such as coordination and understanding instructions. All the staff were extremely helpful. The day was such a success that it lead on to the formation of a trampoline group. Funding was secured from a sports charity to pay for a specialist coach. Each child paid a small sum weekly to cover the hire of the equipment and venue. Ten children attended regularly and the improvements they made were tremendous in a short time.

Setting up the support group has been a success for everyone. No one is an 'expert' in a professional sense but each member is an 'expert' in bringing up a child with this specific learning difficulty, and everyone agrees that this is just the type of 'professional' a parent needs to talk to from time to time.

Contacts

The Dyspraxia Foundation
8 West Alley
Hitchin
Herts
SG5 1EG
Website: www.dyspraxiafoundation.co.uk
Tel: 01462 455016

The Dyscovery Centre
4a Church Road
Whitchurch
Cardiff
CF14 2DZ
Website: www.dyscoverycentre.co.uk
Tel: 02920 628222

Contact a Family
170 Tottenham Court Road
London
W1P 0HA
Website: www.contactafamily.co.uk
Tel: 020 7383 3555

The Voice of the Child

Including contributions from Bridgend County Borough Council

The involvement of pupils in the assessment and management of their own learning needs is an area of development which has seen some progress in more recent years. Since the implementation of the Education Act 1993 and the subsequent publication of the Code of Practice 1994, schools have had to make concerted efforts to readdress their approaches to the management of special educational needs. An area of the revised Code of Practice 2001 which has received less attention is that of pupils' own direct involvement in the assessment and learning process. Paragraph 2:37 of the 1994 Code of Practice states: 'Special educational provision will be most effective when those responsible *take into account* the ascertainable wishes of the child concerned, considered in the light of his or her understanding.' The revised Code of Practice 2001 is much stronger and states that the views of the child *should* be sought and taken into account.

Principles of participation

The ultimate goal for effective pupil participation must be to make participation meaningful and ongoing so that:

- Everyone involved with children and young people commits themselves to the challenge of ensuring pupil participation and making it work.

- There is a long-term commitment to the involvement of pupils.

- Pupils are trained and encouraged to become actively involved.

- Teachers are taught how to involve pupils actively in the decision-making process.

- There is a determination on all sides to make it work.

Teacher training

Involving pupils in the management of their own learning requires a higher order of skills on the part of the teacher. Byers (1994) argues there should be a measured devolution of central control from teachers to pupils. If we are going to move beyond simply valuing opinions from our learners the whole dialogue between pupils and teachers will need to be explored to find out more about what works and doesn't work in order to plan for future needs. Not only might this save the teacher time and make the process more manageable but it is more likely to lead to more accurate judgements about attainments.

Different children, different needs

Recently I spoke to a close friend's son, Michael, who had just finished university where he not only gained a first-class honours degree but was awarded a national prize for an outstanding performance in his chosen area of study. He is now working in London with one of the leading companies in his field. The thing about Michael was that not only did he have a specific learning difficulty but it was only diagnosed when he was at university. One evening we sat down and Michael showed me the report that had been written by the educational psychologist during his first year at university and he began to tell me his story. Clearly this was a pupil with above average intelligence who had managed to get by in school. Asked if he regretted not knowing earlier he was clear that he had not wanted to be treated any differently in school and he had managed through his own personal strategies to overcome any difficulties. The crunch for him came when he was at university and realized his difficulties meant he was not able to order and present his work. Driven by his personal ambitions this was a crossroads and turning point where Michael was prepared to accept the help needed to achieve the goals that would bring him the success he now knew he was capable of.

It was interesting to listen to Michael's case and to the way in which he had assumed control in his school environment. For many other pupils their experience of school has given them a much more negative image of their institution. The snapshot accounts that follow give a few brief descriptions of their plight. Good teacher–student dialogue provides a positive means of working towards greater empowerment for pupils like Michael in their learning environment. I am delighted that the pupils who have contributed to this book to help professionals will have the last word. We know we have a long way to go in getting things right but I believe that listening to the voice of the child is one of the most important ingredients if we are to create an effective learning environment.

My first experience of dyspraxia

I first found out about my dyspraxia when I was in my primary school. I was given a series of physiotherapy sessions to help me.

Now I am in secondary school and the main subjects that I have the most difficulty in is English, history and geography. The main part of my life in secondary school that I have found most difficult is during the exams, but I still manage to complete everything on time.

My friends have helped me by providing the support that I needed. Two of them have dyslexia. They have helped me as they are there for me at times when I needed someone to talk to. It has been really helpful if it was something that I couldn't tell my parents, as it would usually end up in a row over the meaning of dyspraxia.

I have never found it difficult with my friends as I provide them with the same sort of help, by being there for others when they are in need.

The feeling of having coordination difficulties is depressing as it means that I put everyone behind in school work and that they never get good marks because of me. I have now progressed through from year 7, in which my handwriting was made better by my special needs teacher at the time. He gave me a lot of advice and I put the advice to use.

The main thing that has helped me through the school is the thought of being able to get a job as a special needs teacher where I can help others.

Anthony Thompson

Aged 16

Dyspraxia dilemma

My name is Rhian and I am 13. I have dyspraxia. I first found out I had this disability when I was 9. The reason it was discovered was because I was seeing a counsellor for my behavioural problems. Tests were carried out and it was then discovered that I had dyspraxia.

This disability affects my handwriting and also my balance. It causes me to fall over at least once a day, frequently ruining my clothes.

In school I find it difficult copying from the whiteboard and often fall behind with my written tasks. My friends don't really understand, so don't help me and I hate to ask for help because I feel it is embarrassing.

Having coordination difficulties makes me feel left out because none of the other girls in my year have it and can appreciate how I feel or what it's like to deal with this every day.

Rhian Watkins

Aged 13

Pupils' perspectives

Dyspraxia – making it through

I'm Matthew. I am a dyspraxic 14-year-old boy. I first noticed that I had difficulties with things in junior school where I realized I couldn't do my shoelaces up and everyone else could. I started to notice other differences between myself and others like my handwriting wasn't up to their standard and my drawings were very crude.

In school I have problems with a lot of things. My handwriting is awful. My diagrams in science and maths leave a lot to be desired. My throwing and catching skills for PE are very bad. But they all have gotten better since I started attending a motor programme which was set up in my school.

My friends have helped me a lot by giving me support, correcting me when I'm wrong and by taking my mind off my problems. Without them I would have been very stressed out and probably would not have been able to get through if it wasn't for them being there and supporting me.

Sometimes seeing my friends doing stuff that I can't do well upsets me but at the same time I think, 'I may not be able to do that but I can do this and they can't'. This attitude has made me realize that it's not worth worrying about what you can't do and what your friends can do. But you should instead think about what you can do and then work on the skills you want.

Having coordination difficulties makes me slightly upset but I've learnt with enough perseverance you can accomplish anything anyone else can do. I'm not saying it's easy, in fact it's probably a huge challenge to do anything as easily as your friends when you have these difficulties, but when you finally crack it then it's the greatest feeling you can possibly get. I remember the first time I did my shoes up myself (at the age of 9) and it felt really good knowing that I could finally do something that my friends could do with ease.

In school the one thing that has helped me the most is the DCD motor group. We get together on a Monday lunchtime and we do things like throwing and catching exercises and balance along with fun games. All this with other children who have the same problems so there's no name calling or bullying because everyone is in the same boat.

It is very difficult to say who has helped me the most in school because everyone has been so great to me. All of my teachers and friends have supported me in ways they don't even know about but I think the single one person who has helped me the most is probably Mrs Hughes. This lady has selflessly given up her lunch hour and spare time to help children like me get around the problems they face in everyday life. In my opinion this lady deserves a medal for the things she puts up with and still manages to stay sane.

Matthew Danter-Lawson

Aged 14

Caged in chaos

For many years Vicky Biggs was haunted by the feeling that there was something wrong with her. She fell over a lot. She was useless at games or anything that required physical coordination. She had no friends. Yet from the age of 3 she could read fluently and, although her grades at school were often mediocre, she knew that there were many concepts she understood instantly where her peers struggled.

'It was very confusing because I knew I was different,' she says. 'I knew I was clumsy, a bit antisocial, but the problem areas are very diverse so I was never able to work out what was wrong. It was like having a small volcano sitting inside me. Also, some of my better attributes, like the photographic memory, I assumed everyone had them. The realisation came in fragments.'

Her condition, dyspraxia, was not diagnosed until she was 15, and this was a liberating experience. Not only did she discover that her lack of physical coordination puts her in the bottom 1 percent of the population, but a psychologist told her that her IQ, at 155, is in the top 1 percent. Suddenly her behaviour made sense because she knew why she struggled to organise the way she moves: her brain isn't wired like most people and when it tries to send messages not all of them get through. So she has poor balance and depth perception – she can reach for a door handle and miss, she can't pour a drink without spilling, or walk upstairs without hanging on to something. She struggles to cross roads because she can't judge the speed of traffic and, in spite of six years of weekly piano lessons, she has yet to reach Grade 1.

Vicky grew up in Saudi Arabia where her father works for an aeronautic company and her mother is a midwife; it was there that the bullying started and eventually became intolerable. 'The bullying has pretty much always gone on. The only thing being I usually have my head in the clouds so I don't notice if someone's being horrible unless it's pointed out to me. It's only if people are pushing me around that I can tell.'

When she was 12 and moved to a new school in the Hijax Mountains the taunts accelerated. She was called 'Spaz,' 'Reject,' 'Retard,' and other names she will not repeat. Her books were stolen and torn; she was pushed down the stairs. 'It was things like ... they knew I had a phobia of spiders so there would be spiders in my desk, sand in my apple juice.'

Having dyspraxia is, she says, like 'lying diagonally in a parallel universe' and it feels like a cage. Or rather it did. Apart from reacting to the diagnosis by wanting to shout 'I'm not a freak!' Vicky rapidly became more confident. A clear sign of this is the book she has written, *Caged in Chaos: A Dyspraxic Guide to Breaking Free* (ISBN: 020 78332 307), which is primarily a practical guide to living with the condition, but also a way of explaining herself to those who, for the first 15 years of her life, thought her stupid.

Victoria Biggs

(Extract taken from *The Times* 2.3.05)

Useful Websites for children with dyspraxia can be found on: www.darlen.co.uk/dyspraxicteen

My day

I get up in the morning

My head's in a spin

I don't want to get up

Don't want the day to begin

I have my breakfast

and get myself dressed

Sometimes my clothes go on wrong

but I try my best

My mum takes me to school

I go off to my class

I struggle through my work

I wish the time would pass

My writing is messy

My drawings are too

I'm no good at PE

I can't even do up my shoe

I wish my life wasn't this hard

I wish it was more fun

I wish nobody laughed at me

The race is over before I've begun

I'd like to play more sports

But I'm never picked for teams

I wish I could be better

Like I am in my dreams

Catharine Jones

Aged 9

References and further reading

Chapter 1 Children with development coordination disorder: setting the scene

Ainscow, M. (1999) *Understanding the Development of Inclusive Schools*. London: Routledge Falmer.

American Psychiatric Association (1994) *Diagnostic and Statistical Manual of Mental Disorders* (DSM IV), 4th edn. Washington, DC: American Psychiatric Association.

Brenner, M.W. and Gilman, S. (1967) 'Visuo-motor disability in school children', *British Medical Journal*, 4, 259–62.

Cantell, M.H., Smyth, M.M. and Ahonen, T.P. (1994) 'Clumsiness in adolescence. Educational, motor and social outcomes of motor delay detected at 5 years', *Adapted Physical Activity Quarterly*, 11, 115–29.

Dare, M.T. and Gordon, N. (1970) 'Clumsy children: a disorder of perception and motor organisation', *Developmental Medicine and Child Neurology*, 12, 178–85.

Department for Education and Skills (2001) *Special Educational Needs and Disability Rights Act*. London: HMSO.

Department for Education and Skills (2001) *Special Educational Needs Code of Practice*. London: HMSO.

Gardner, H. (1999) *The Disciplined Mind*. London: Simon & Schuster.

Godfrey, K. (1994) 'Clumsy, not clots', *She* magazine, August.

Gordon, N. and McKinlay, I. (1980) *Helping Clumsy Children*. New York: Churchill Livingstone.

Gubbay, S.S. (1975) *The Clumsy Child – A Study of Apraxia and Agnostic Ataxia*. London: Saunders.

Henderson, S.E. and Barnett, A.L. (1998) 'The classification of specific motor co-ordination disorders: some problems to be solved', *Human Movement Science*, 17, 449–69.

Henderson, S.E. and Hall, D. (1982) 'Concomitants of clumsiness in young school children', *Developmental Medicine and Child Neurology*, 24, 448–60.

Henderson, S. and Sugden, D. (1992) *Movement Assessment Battery for Children*. Sidcup, Kent.

Iloeje, S.O. (1987) 'Developmental apraxia among Nigerian children in Enugor, Nigeria', *Dev. Med. Child Neurol.*, 29, 502–7.

Jones, N. (2002) *The Role of the Senco in the Primary School*. MA dissertation, University of Wales.

Kaplan, B.J., Crawford, S.G., Wilson, B.N., Dewey, D.M. (1998) 'DCD may not be a discrete disorder', *Human Movement Science*, 17, 471–90.

Law, J., Lindsay, G., Peacey, N. and Soloff, N. (2001) 'Facilitating communication between education and health services: the provision for children with speech and language needs', *British Journal of Special Educational Needs*, 28, 23.

Losen, S. and Losen, J. (1985) *The Special Education Team*. Boston: Allyn & Bacon.

Marks, K. (1994) 'The hidden disorder of a clumsy child', *Daily Telegraph*, 13 January.

Morris, P.R. and Whiting, H.T.A. (1971) *Motor Impairment and Compensatory Education*. Philadelphia: Lea & Tefiger.

National Association for Paediatric Occupational Therapists (NAPOT) (2003) *Doubly Disadvantaged. Report of a survey on waiting lists and waiting times for children with DCD*. NAPOT.

Peters, J. and Wright, A. (1999) 'Development and evaluation of a group physical activity programme for children with DCD: an interdisciplinary approach', *Physiotherapy Theory and Practice*, 15, 203–16.

Portwood, M. (1996) *Developmental Dyspraxia. A Practical Manual for Parents and Professionals*. Durham: Durham County Council.

Schoemaker, M.M. and Kalverboer, A.F. (1994) 'Social and affective problems of children who are clumsy: how early do they begin?', *Adapted Physical Activity Quarterly*, 11, 130–40.

Stott, D.H., Moyes, F.A. and Henderson, S.E. (1984) *Test of Motor Impairments*. London: Psychological Corporation.

Sugden, D. and Sugden, L. (1991) 'The assessment of movement skill problems in 7 and 9 year old children', *British Journal of Educational Psychology*, 61, 329–45.

Sugden, D. and Wright, H. (1996) 'Curricular entitlement and implementation for all children', in N. Armstrong (ed.), *New Directions in Physical Education: Change in Innovation*. London: Cassell.

Teacher Training Agency (2001) *National Standards for Qualified Teacher Status*. London: Teacher Training Agency.

Thomas, G. (1997) 'Inclusive schools for an inclusive society', *British Journal of Special Education*, 24 (3), 103–97.

United Nations Education, Scientific and Cultural Organization (1994) *The Salamenca Statement and Framework for Action on Special Needs Education*. UNESCO.

Van Dellen, T. and Geuze, R.H. (1988) 'Motor response processing in clumsy children', *Journal of Child Psychology and Psychiatry*, 29, 489–500.

World Health Organization (1992) *International Classification of Diseases [ICD 10]*, 10th edn. Geneva: WHO.

Wright, H.C. (1997) 'Children with DCD – a review', *European Journal of Physical Education*, 2, 5–22.

Wright, H.C. and Sugden, D.A. (1995) 'Management of children aged 6–9 years with DCD', *Proceedings of the 10th International Symposium on Adapted Physical Activity: DS10*, 22–27 May.

Chapter 2 Specific learning difficulties: the spectrum

American Psychiatric Association (1994) *Diagnostic and Statistical Manual of Mental Disorders* (DSM IV), 4th edn. Washington, DC: APA.

Biedermanet, J., Faraone, S.V., Kennan, K., Knee, D. and Tsuang, M.T. (1990) 'Family Genetic and psychosocial risk factors in DSM-III attention deficit disorder', *Journal of the American Academy of Child and Adolescent Psychiatry*, 29: 526–33.

BPS (1999) *Dyslexia and Psychological Assessment. Report of a Working Party*. Leicester: BPS.

Conners, C.K. (1996) *Conners Rating Scales Revised*. London: Psychological Corporation.

Fawcett, A.J. (2004) *Dyslexia and Learning*. Paper presented at the IDA Conference Philadelphia, USA, November.

Fawcett, A.J. and Nicolson, R.I. (1996) *The Dyslexia Screening Test*. London: Psychological Corporation.

Fawcett, A.J. and Nicolson, R.I. (2004) 'Dyslexia: the role of the cerebellum', in G. Reid and A.J. Fawcett (eds), *Dyslexia in Context; Research, Policy and Practice*. London: Whurr Publications.

Frith, U. (2002) 'Resolving the paradoxes of dyslexia', in G. Reid and J. Wearmouth (eds), *Dyslexia and Literacy, Theory and Practice*. Chichester: Wiley.

Geuze, R.H., Jongmans, M.J., Schoemaker, M.M. and Smits-Engelsman, B.C. (2001) 'Clinical and research diagnostic criteria for developmental coordination disorder: a review and discussion', *Human Movement Science*, 20, 12, 7–47.

Henderson, A., Came, F., and Brough, M. (2003) *Working with Dyscalculia*. Marlborough: Learning Works International.

Kaplan, B.J., Wilson, B.N., Dewey, D. and Crawford, S.G. (1998) 'DCD may not be a discrete disorder', *Human Movement Science*, 17, 471–90.

Lloyd, G. and Norris, C. (1999) 'Including ADHD?', *Disability and Society*, 14 (4), 505–17.

McIntyre, C. and Deponio, P. (2003) *Identifying and Supporting Children with Specific Learning Difficulties – Looking beyond the label to assess the whole child*. London: Routledge Falmer.

Missiuna, C. (1996) *Keeping Current on Developmental Coordination Disorder*. Hamilton, Ont.: Centre for Childhood Disability Research.

Morton, J. and Frith, U. (1995) 'Causal modelling: a structural approach to developmental psychopathology', in D. Cicchetti and D.J. Cohen (eds), *Manual of Developmental Psychopathology*. NY Psychological Assessment of Dyslexia: Wiley.

Portwood, M. (1999) *Developmental Dyspraxia: Identification and Intervention. A Manual for Parents and Professionals*. London: David Fulton.

Portwood, M. (2000) *Understanding Developmental Dyspraxia. A Textbook for Students and Professionals*. London: David Fulton.

Portwood, M. (2004) 'Dyspraxia', in A. Lewis and B. Norwich (eds), *Special Teaching for Special Children*, Pedagogies for Inclusion. Oxford University Press/McGraw-Hill Education.

Ramus, F., Pidgeon, E. and Frith, U. (2003) 'The relationship between motor control and phonology in dyslexic children', *Journal of Child Psychology and Psychiatry and Allied Disciplines*, 44, 712–22.

Rasmussen, P. and Gillberg, I.C. (2000) 'Natural outcome of ADHD with developmental coordination disorder at age 22 years: a controlled longitudinal community-based study', *Journal of American Academy of Child and Adolescent Psychiatry*, 39, 111, 1424–31.

Reason, R. (2002) 'From assessment to intervention: the educational perspective', in G. Reid and J. Wearmouth (eds), *Dyslexia and Literacy, Theory and Practice*. Chichester: Wiley.

Ripley, K. (2001) *Inclusion for Children with Dyspraxia/DCD: A Handbook for Teachers*. London: David Fulton.

Weedon, C. and Reid, G. (2002) *Special Needs Assessment Portfolio*, Pilot version. Edinburgh: George Watsons College.

Weedon, C. and Reid, G. (2003) *Special Needs Assessment Portfolio*. London: Hodder & Stoughton.

Chapter 4 Assessing pupils with coordination difficulties

Bailey, R.P. (1999) 'Physical Education: action, play, movement', in J. Riley and R. Prentice (eds), *The Primary Curriculum 7–11*. London: Chapman.

Bailey, R.P. (2001) *Teaching Physical Education: A Handbook for Primary and Secondary Teachers*. London: Kogan Page.

Black, P. and Wiliam, D. (1998) *'Inside the Black Box': Raising Standards through Classroom Assessment*. London: Nelson.

Buschner, C. (1994) *Teaching Children Movement Concepts and Skills*. Champaign, IL: Human Kinetics.

Capel, S. (2001) *Learning to Teach Physical Education in the Secondary School*. London. Routledge.

Capel, S. (2004) *Learning to Teach Physical Education in the Secondary School*. London: Routledge.

Carroll, B. (1994) *Assessment in Physical Education: A Teacher's Guide to the Issues*. London: Falmer.

Chambers, H. and Sugden, D. (2003) *Early Years Movement Skills: Description, Diagnosis and Intervention*. London: Whurr Publications.

Cheminais, R. (2001) *Developing Inclusive School: A Practical Guide*. London: Fulton.

DfES (2001) *Special Educational Needs Code of Practice*. London: HMSO.

DfES (2002) *Ofsted Report: Assessment in Physical Education*. London: HMSO.

Frapwell, A., Glass, C. and Pearce, L. (2002) 'Assessment "work in progress"', *British Journal of Teaching Physical Education*, 33, 3, 23–5.

Harlen, W., Gipps, C., Broadfoot, P. and Nuttall, D. (1994) 'Assessment and the improvement of education', in B. Moon and A.S. Mayes (eds), *Teaching and Learning in the Secondary School*. London: Routledge.

Henderson, S.E. and Sugden, D.A. (1992) *Movement Assessment Battery for Children*. London: Psychological Corporation.

Laban, R. (1942) *The Mastery of Movement*, 4th edn. London: McDonald & Evans.

Macfadyen, T.M. and Bailey, R.P. (2002) *Teaching Physical Education 11–18*. London: Continuum.

Macintyre, C. (2000) *Dyspraxia in the Early Years*. London: Fulton.

Peach, S. and Bamforth, C. (2002) 'Tackling the problems of assessment, recording and reporting in physical education and Initial Teacher Training', *British Journal of Teaching Physical Education*, 33, 2, 19–22.

Piotrowski, S. (2000) 'Assessment, recording and reporting', in R.P. Bailey and T.M. Macfadyen (eds), *Teaching Physical Education 5–11*. London: Continuum.

Ripley, K., Davies, B. and Barrett, J. (1997) 'Dyspraxia': A Guide for Teachers and Parents. London: Fulton.

Stillwell, J.L. and Wilgoose, C.E. (1997) The Physical Education Curriculum, 5th edn. Needham Heights, MA: Allyn & Bacon.

Sugden, D. and Wright, H. (1996) 'Curricular entitlement and implementation for all children', in N. Armstrong (ed.), New Directions in Physical Education: Change and Innovation. London: Cassell.

Sugden, D. and Wright, H. (1998) Motor Coordination Disorder in Children. Thousand Oaks, CA: Sage.

Sugden, D., Wright, H., Chambers, M. and Markee, A. (1993) Developmental Coordination Disorder: A Booklet for Parents and Professionals. Leeds: Leeds University Press.

Vickerman, P. (1997) 'Knowing your pupils and planning for different need', in S. Capel (ed.), Learning to Teach in the Secondary School. London: Routledge.

Winnick, J.P. (2000) Adapted Physical Education and Sport, 3rd edn. Champaign, IL: Human Kinetics

Chapter 6 Developing a gross motor programme for children with coordination difficulties

Cowden, J.E. and Eusson, B.L. (1991) 'Paediatric adapted physical education for infants, toddlers and pre-school children', Adapted Physical Education Quarterly, 8, 263–79.

Keen, D. (2001) Specific Neurodevelopmental Disorders. Paper presented at the Conference on the Needs of Children with Specific Developmental Difficulties, Bishop Aukland, March.

Macintyre, C. (2003) Jingle Time: Rhymes and Activities for Early Years' Learning. London: David Fulton.

Macintyre, C. and Deponio, P. (2003) Assessing and Supporting Children with Specific Learning Difficulties. Looking Beyond the Label to Assess the Whole Child. London: Routledge.

Chapter 7 Adapting the PE curriculum

Ainscow, M., Farrell, D., Tweedle, D. and Malkin, G. (1999) Effective Practice in Inclusion and in Special and Mainstream Schools Working Together. London: HMSO.

Department for Education and Skills (2001) Special Educational Needs and Disability Rights Act. London: HMSO.

Department for Education and Skills (2001) Special Educational Needs Code of Practice. London: HMSO:

Department for Education and Skills (2003) Success For All – An inclusive approach to PE and school sport. CD-ROM resource available from: dfes@prolog.uk.com.

Department of Education (1988) The Education Reform Act. London: HMSO.

Department of Education and the Welsh Office (1992) Physical Education for Ages 5 to 16. Final Report of the National Curriculum Physical Education Working Group. London: HMSO:

Dyson, A. (1999) 'Examining Issues of Inclusion'. Unpublished paper, Department of Education, University of Newcastle.

Index